The
BUSINESS
of GAY
WEDDINGS
&

A GUIDE FOR
WEDDING PROFESSIONALS

BERNADETTE COVENEY SMITH

This edition was printed in 2013 by Goodnow Flow Publishing

The Business of Gay Weddings: A Guide for Wedding Professionals

Copyright ©2013 by Bernadette Coveney Smith.

ISBN
PAPERBACK - 978-0-615-88925-2

Cover & Book design by Ian Berg

DEDICATION

To all the wonderful LGBTQ clients who have come into my life because of 14 Stories, I thank you for being boldly yourselves, for making history and for inspiring my life and my work.

TABLE OF CONTENTS

PREFACE

Marriage equality in the United States and around the world is accelerating rapidly. It's been nearly a decade since I started my wedding planning company, 14 Stories, back when same-sex marriage became legal in Massachusetts. It was lonely for a while, but since November 2012 to the time of print, sixteen states (California, Connecticut, Delaware, Iowa, Maine, Maryland, Massachusetts, Minnesota, New Hampshire, New York, Rhode Island, Vermont, Washington, New Jersey, Hawaii and Illinois) and the District of Columbia have legalized same-sex marriage. By the time you read this, same-sex marriage may even be legal in New Jersey, Hawaii and Oregon!

This is amazing progress for same-sex couples – but it's also amazing news for the wedding industry. Same-sex marriage is here and the wedding industry needs to catch up and get ready to reach this powerful, lucrative emerging market. Gay weddings are FUN and will bring new energy to your business. I know that I absolutely love what I do.

As you read through this book, I'll share lots of anecdotes and examples from my business over the years – you may find some of these stories crazy but I promise I don't make this stuff up! It's amazing what people say sometimes.

Also – I want to introduce you to my family – my wife Jen and my son, Patrick. Jen and I married in 2009 in Boston and Patrick was born on October 31, 2010 (yes, a Halloween baby!) I mention them because a lot of the things I talk about in this book affect my family, particularly all the details I share about the laws. So while this book is practical, useful and hopefully an enjoyable read, it's also personal for me.

And finally, you'll notice I use the phrase "gay weddings" more than any other in this book. I am using that to keep things simple, as an umbrella term for the LGBTQ community, not to alienate anyone who is LBTor Q!

If you, like many in the wedding industry, are used to only one bride and one groom, then this book is for you. Go forth and prosper with these joyful weddings!

CHAPTER 1

A Brief History Lesson

Gay, lesbian, bisexual, and transgender people have always been a part of world history and culture. While aspects of these identities are unique to the 20th century, it is crucial to know that LGBT experiences have always been an essential part of the development of human sexuality and relationships across global histories and cultures.

You may wonder why this is important to you in the wedding industry. See, while there has been huge progress made towards marriage equality, there are still millions of Americans and many millions more around the world who think being gay is a choice and being gay is a sin. You may encounter some of those people in your experiences planning same-sex weddings. So here's some background on LGBT history so you can speak with even greater confidence about the LGBT community.

During the 20th century, cultural attitudes towards sex and sexuality swung wildly between extremes. In the early 20th century, Freud's psychological theories of sexuality and the Modernist literary and artistic movements created a widespread cultural acknowledgment of the existence of bisexuality and homosexuality, even if the acceptance of these identities were limited to bohemian and avant-garde subcultures. However, during WWII, the Nazis sent homosexuals along with the Jews to the concentration camps.

In the 1950s, the Kinsey Report was a watershed moment in mainstream understanding of sexuality and the actual sexual practices of Americans. However, very few people could live openly with same-sex partners, and most gay and lesbian Americans lived in silence with the ever-present fear of criminalization. All fifty states had sodomy laws that were used as the justification for constant surveillance and raids on gay bars. It was not unusual for people to be arrested for simply being in a gay bar, and many people were brutally and physically harassed once arrested and in custody.

In June 1969, the Stonewall Riots in New York City's Greenwich Village marked the beginning of the contemporary gay rights movement. Police raided the Stonewall Inn for catering to openly gay patrons, and the patrons subsequently responded by rioting. This revolt was a very significant moment in history, because it was the first time that a collective action against police harassment and legal discrimination against the gay community had ever taken place. A year later, 5,000 people took to the streets of Manhattan to march and commemorate the events at Stonewall. This march soon became known as the Pride Parade, which now takes place annually in cities all over the country. Pride Parades are a joyous celebration of living openly and authentically.

The LGBT civil rights movement has accelerated since Stonewall. Anti-sodomy laws were eventually struck down by the Supreme Court. Twenty-two states now have anti-discrimination policies that include sexual orientation and/or gender identity. Don't Ask Don't Tell, the law banning openly gay military members, was struck down. The federal Defense of Marriage Act was overturned, allowing for federal recognition of same-sex marriage. And of course there is a great deal of marriage equality momentum.

A TIMELINE OF
MARRIAGE EQUALITY
IN THE UNITED STATES

 1970   **1975**   **1991**

• Jack Baker and Michael McConnell applied for a marriage license in Hennepin County, Minnesota. After being turned down, Baker and McConnell obtained a marriage license from another Minnesota county. A Methodist minister officiated in a marriage ceremony in Minneapolis and executed the license.

• Two men from Phoenix, Arizona are granted a marriage license by their county clerk. The Arizona Supreme Court would later invalidate the license. Two months later, in Colorado, county Clerk Clela Rorex issued six marriage licenses to same-sex couples. The state DA's office later issued an opinion that the licenses were invalid and no new licenses were issued.

• Fox's comedy drama series Roc depicted the first same-sex marriage on American TV. Uncle Russell marries his partner.

1993   **1998**   **1999**

• The Hawaii State Supreme Court rules in Baehr v. Lewin that the Hawaii state statute limiting marriage to oppositee-sex couples is presumed to be unconstitutional unless the state can present a "compelling state interest" justifying the same sex marriage ban.

• Roy and Silo, two male Chinstrap Penguins, are observed performing mating rituals. They were eventually given an egg to hatch and raised Tango, a female penguin.

• Governor Gray Davis from the US state of California signs a registered partnerships bill into law that provided limited rights for same-sex couples.

• Two women, both named Kimberly, were chosen by visitors to TheKnot.com as The Knot Millennium Couple, winning a prize package worth nearly $5000.

A TIMELINE OF
MARRIAGE EQUALITY
IN THE UNITED STATES

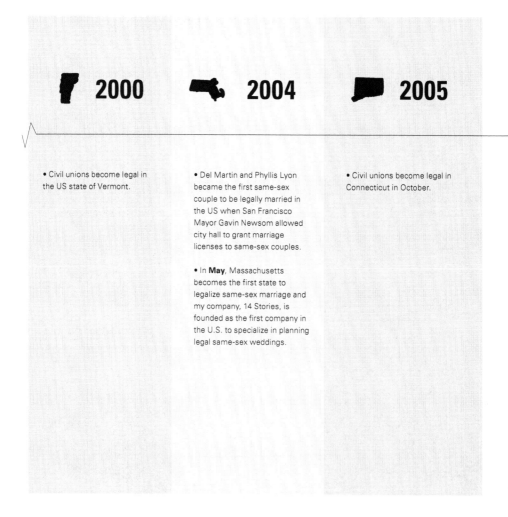

2000

- Civil unions become legal in the US state of Vermont.

2004

- Del Martin and Phyllis Lyon became the first same-sex couple to be legally married in the US when San Francisco Mayor Gavin Newsom allowed city hall to grant marriage licenses to same-sex couples.

- In **May**, Massachusetts becomes the first state to legalize same-sex marriage and my company, 14 Stories, is founded as the first company in the U.S. to specialize in planning legal same-sex weddings.

2005

- Civil unions become legal in Connecticut in October.

2008

 2009

 2010

• Marriage begins in California in May after a California Supreme Court ruling. By November 3rd, more than 18,000 same-sex couples have married. However, on November 4, California voters approved a ban on same-sex marriage called Proposition 8. Those 18,000 marriages remained valid.

• Marriage begins in Connecticut in October.

• Marriage begins in Vermont in April.

• On May 6, the governor of Maine legalized same-sex marriage in that state in **Maine**; however, citizens voted to overturn that law when they went to the polls in November, and Maine became the 31st state to ban the practice.

• Couple Jeremy Hooper and Andrew Shulman are featured in the June edition of Martha Stewart Weddings magazine.

• Marriage begins in New Hampshire as of January 1.

Marriage is legalized in the District of Columbia.

A TIMELINE OF
MARRIAGE EQUALITY
IN THE UNITED STATES

 **2011**   **2012**  **2013**

• Marriage is legalized in New York State in July.

• In February, Washington becomes the seventh state to legalize gay marriage.

• In March, Maryland passes legislation to legalize gay marriage, becoming the eighth state.

• In May, Barack Obama becomes the first sitting U.S. president to publicly announce support for same-sex marriage. "It is important for me to go ahead and affirm that I think same-sex couples should be able to get married," he said.

• Same-sex marriage is on the November ballot for Maine, Maryland, Washington, and Minnesota and voters in all four states support marriage equality, the first time voters have ever done so.

• The United States Supreme Court struck down the Defense of Marriage Act on June 26. Through the case Hollingsworth v. Perry, the Court dismissed the Proposition 8 appeal, which leaves the ruling of the district court in effect, nullifying the amendment and rendering same-sex marriage legal again in California.

• Same-sex marriage begins in New Jersey in October and Hawaii in December. The law passes in Illinois, to begin in 2014.

• The Knot releases a digital same-sex marriage magazine, one featuring stories from real brides and one from real grooms. The digital magazine can be downloaded at:

IN SUMMARY

We've made some great progress with marriage equality though there is much work to do. Check out this map so you can see which countries around the world offer freedom to marry:

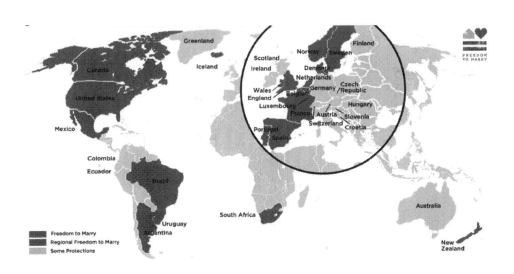

CHAPTER 2

LGBT What?

Let's start with some definitions. I'll be using these terms throughout the book so I'd like you to get familiar with them now.

TERMS DESCRIBING WHO YOU LOVE

Sexual Orientation: Describes an individual's physical, romantic, emotional, and/or spiritual attraction to members of the same and/or opposite sex. Terms include heterosexual, gay, lesbian, bisexual, and queer.

Lesbian: A woman whose physical, romantic, emotional, and/or spiritual attraction is to other women.

Bisexual: An individual who is physically, romantically, emotionally, and/or spiritually attracted to men and women. Bisexuals need not have had equal sexual experience with both men and women; in fact, they need not have had any sexual experience at all to identify as bisexual.

Gay: Describes people whose enduring physical, romantic, emotional, and/or spiritual attractions are to people of the same sex. The term is often used to refer to gay men, but it can be used to encompass all genders.

Heterosexual: A person whose enduring physical, romantic, emotional, and/or spiritual attraction is to people of the opposite sex.

LGBT(Q): An acronym meaning lesbian, gay, bisexual, transgender, and queer and the most inclusive term used to describe this group. Sometimes "Q" means "Questioning, not "Queer." Sometimes written as GLBT.

TERMS DESCRIBING WHO YOU ARE

Sex: Biological gender assigned at birth. Infants are labeled either male or female based on a combination of bodily characteristics including: chromosomes, hormones, internal reproductive organs, and genitals.

Gender Identity: An individual's internal sense and experience of gender. Includes male, female, transgender, genderqueer, queer, and more. For transgender people, their birth-assigned sex and their own internal sense of gender identity do not match.

Gender Expression: External manifestation of one's gender identity, expressed through "masculine," "feminine," or gender-variant behavior, clothing, haircut, voice, or body characteristics. Transgender people usually want their gender expression to match their gender identity rather than their birth-assigned sex.

Transgender: An umbrella term for people whose gender identity and/or gender expression differs from the sex that they were assigned at birth. Transgender people may or may not decide to alter their bodies hormonally and/or surgically.

MTF: A transgender person who was born male but identifies as female. Also known as a transwoman.

FTM: A transgender person who was born female but identifies as male. Also known as a transman.

Transition: Altering one's birth sex is not a one-step procedure; it is a complex process that occurs over a long period of time. Transition includes some or all of the following cultural, legal, and medical adjustments: telling one's family, friends, and/or co-workers; changing one's name and/or sex on legal documents; hormone therapy; and possibly (though not always) some form of surgical alteration.

Sex Reassignment Surgery: Refers to surgical alteration, which is only one small part of transition. Preferred term to "sex change operation." Not all transgender people choose to or can afford to have SRS.

Cross-Dressing: To occasionally wear clothes traditionally associated with people of the other sex. Cross-dressers are usually comfortable with the sex they were assigned at birth and do not wish to change it. Cross-dresser should NOT be used to describe someone who has transitioned to live full-time as the other sex or who intends to do so in the future. That term would be transgender. Cross-dressing is a form of gender expression and is not necessarily tied to erotic activity, nor is it indicative of sexual orientation.

Intersex: Describes a person whose biological sex is ambiguous. There are many genetic, hormonal, or anatomical variations that make a person's sex ambiguous (e.g., Klinefelter Syndrome, Adrenal Hyperplasia). Parents and medical professionals usually assign intersex infants a sex and perform surgical operations to conform the infant's body to that assignment. This practice has become increasingly controversial as intersex adults are speaking out against the practice.

Butch: A lesbian with a more masculine gender expression and appearance.

'Bridegroom' Peaches hugs new bride after ceremony.

Bridegroom: An engaged lesbian who may not feel comfortable using the term bride. Often someone who is more butch or boyish in appearance. First seen in popular culture in a 1970 issue of Jet magazine.

One thing you may have noticed in the definitions is that gender and sexuality are fluid. There are not just two boxes: STRAIGHT and GAY. There are many people who fall somewhere in between. Similarly, there are not just two boxes for gender: MALE and FEMALE. Many people identify somewhere in the middle. It's important to embrace this fluidity so you don't accidentally offend a couple who doesn't fit neatly into a box.

The Genderbread Person

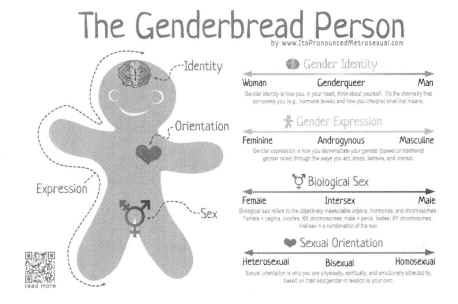

by www.ItsPronouncedMetrosexual.com

Gender Identity

Woman — Genderqueer — Man

Gender identity is how you, in your head, think about yourself. It's the chemistry that composes you (e.g., hormone levels) and how you interpret what that means.

Gender Expression

Feminine — Androgynous — Masculine

Gender expression is how you demonstrate your gender (based on traditional gender roles) through the ways you act, dress, behave, and interact.

Biological Sex

Female — Intersex — Male

Biological sex refers to the objectively measurable organs, hormones, and chromosomes. Female = vagina, ovaries, XX chromosomes; male = penis, testes, XY chromosomes; intersex = a combination of the two.

Sexual Orientation

Heterosexual — Bisexual — Homosexual

Sexual orientation is who you are physically, spiritually, and emotionally attracted to, based on their sex/gender in relation to your own.

read more

As you are meeting with a couple, you may want to determine what language makes them comfortable. I know this is a burning question because it's one of the common e-mails I get: how do I refer to my clients? Here are some examples of how to proceed:

Bad example

Wedding planner: It's so great to meet you! So, is one of you the bride and one of you the groom in this relationship?

Couple: Um, no we're both the grooms.

Bad example

Wedding planner: It's so great to meet you! So, is one of you the bride and one of you the groom in this relationship?

Couple: Um, no. We don't have roles like that.

Good example

Wedding planner: It's so great to meet you! Are you comfortable being referred to as the grooms or is there another term you prefer?

Couple: Grooms is fine, thanks!

Good example

Wedding planner: It's so great to meet you! Are you comfortable being referred to as the brides or is there another term you prefer? I know some women prefer the term bridegrooms.

Couple: Thanks for asking. Melissa is definitely the bride but I feel more like a bridegroom.

BE CAREFUL WITH THESE TERMS

Queer: Traditionally a pejorative term, it has been appropriated by some LGBT people to describe themselves. Some value the term for its defiance, and because it can be inclusive of the entire LGBT community. Nevertheless, it is not universally accepted even within the LGBT community and should be avoided unless quoting someone who self-identifies that way. It is much more common among younger generations, because they identify with its emphasis on fluidity and non-normative sexualities and genders.

Homosexual: Outdated clinical term considered derogatory and offensive by many gay people. Because of the clinical history of the word "homosexual," it has been adopted by anti-gay extremists to suggest that lesbians and gay men are somehow diseased or psychologically/emotionally disordered notions discredited by both the American Psychological Association and the American Psychiatric Association in the 1970s.

Lifestyle (also known as "alternative lifestyle"): Inaccurate term often used by anti-gay extremists to denigrate lesbian, gay, bisexual, and transgender lives. As there is no one heterosexual or straight lifestyle, there is no one lesbian, gay, bisexual, or transgender lifestyle.

Transsexual: An antiquated term that originated in the medical and psychological communities. It has subsequently been replaced by the term transgender.

Transvestite: Old, and now derogatory term for people who cross-dress. The appropriate term is cross-dresser.

Sexual Preference: A term used to suggest that being lesbian, gay or bisexual is a choice and therefore can and should be "cured."

LGBT SUBCULTURES

As with all large identity groups, you can find smaller groups (called subcultures) within the larger groups. Subcultures form when groups of people bond over shared interests or aesthetics. Within the LGBTQ community, you can find many different kinds of subcultures. Examples include:

• leather bears (husky, bearded, mustached gay men who are into leather)
• polyamory (having non-monogamous committed relationships with more than one person)
• granola lesbians (earthy, eco-conscious, all-natural)
• boi-culture (FTMs with an adolescent boy aesthetic)
• high-femmes (super feminine women)
• drag queens (men who impersonate and perform as women often celebrities)
• drag kings (women who impersonate and perform as men)
• queens (flamboyant and bitchy gay men)

I'll never forget one of our company's very first weddings, back in 2004. It was a wedding of two leather bears, and they were enthusiastic about showcasing bear pride at their wedding. We started off with teddy bear themed wedding invitations and stationery. We had teddy bear figurines as cake topper and instead of a bouquet toss, had a teddy bear toss. The guests got a kick out of it and of course the grooms felt like they could fully be themselves. It was a playful way to personalize their wedding.

A few weeks ago, I was at a networking event catching up with a wedding planner who had gone through my training for wedding professionals. She was telling me about her first gay wedding client and how, through my training, she was able to be sensitive to the couple's unique needs. And unique they were. The planner mentioned that I never said anything in my training about a trio. And I'm not talking about a string or a jazz trio!

This particular couple mentioned that there would be several trios at the wedding. They were referring not to a couple, but a threesome, and not just a sexual threesome, but a relationship trio all committed to each other.

At first this planner was thrown off, but she ultimately rolled with it, and that's what you have to do. Be open-minded, non-judgmental, and professional—and everyone will be happy. Your clients will have their dream wedding, and you will reap the benefits of new and happy clientele!

BE CAREFUL WITH STEREOTYPES

We may want to argue that stereotypes don't come out of thin air, right? There is something to that association between drag queen and gay man, or the link between hip-hop and African American youth. Below are some stereotypes you may encounter, either in your own beliefs or in mainstream culture, about LGBT people and same-sex weddings:

Gay men
- Drag queen
- Flamboyant
- In a couple, one is the "male" and one is the "female"
- Will want to wear a wedding dress
- Will want to wear makeup
- Promiscuous/won't settle down
- Make a lot of money
- Won't need a wedding planner because they'll plan their own lavish affair

Lesbians
- Couple up very quickly (U-Haul joke)
- In a couple, one is the "male" and one is the "female"
- One will wear a tux and one will wear a wedding dress
- Lesbians are cheap
- Lesbians hate men
- Don't wear make up or care about fashion
- Tend to be vegetarians and vegans

Bisexuals
- Bisexuals can't make up their minds/are confused
- Being bi is a temporary feeling or fleeting phase
- Bisexuals just want to have sex all the time
- When a bisexual person gets married, he or she has chosen a "team"

Transgender People
- You can always tell a transgender person—something is just not quite normal
- A transgender person's sexuality is determined by the gender of the person they are with
- They are usually drag queens
- A transgender person will end up having a "straight" wedding because they were gay to begin with, and changing their gender means they are now heterosexual.

Are there gay men who are drag queens and love to plan lavish events? Of course. Are there vegan lesbians who are in a butch/femme relationship? Certainly. Are there bisexuals with high sex drives? You betcha. Can our transgender radar often be on target? Sure. So what is the difference between these actual people and the stereotypes?

Stereotypes are logical fallacies of generalization. For instance, some tomatoes are red, juicy, and delicious. Therefore, all tomatoes are red, juicy, and delicious. What happens if you encounter a delicious red tomato that is not juicy? Or what if you find yourself surrounded by yellow, heirloom, and green tomatoes? Stereotypes simplify, limit, and box your encounter with an individual. Stereotypes are lazy. Why get to know any gay man if you already know all about gay men? Often, stereotypes are a technique deployed by powerful groups onto less powerful groups, because stereotypes usually have negative connotations.

For example, here is another way to look at the stereotype of lesbians being cheap: statistically, two women in a couple will make significantly less money and have significantly less wealth than two men in a couple because of the gender wage gap and the low-paying "pink collar" industries. Therefore, the two women may have less disposable income and may be less likely to spend it on entertainment or partying. How does this present a different version of the same idea? At the same time, this fact about the gender wage gaps should not be used to harden an assumption. The lesbian community portrayed on Showtime's The L Word is made up of high-earning, successful women, and many lesbians in the real world have high incomes.

Stereotypes harm interpersonal and professional interactions. As you move through the rest of the unit, think about how stereotypes and assumptions could obstruct your goals for workplace and client diversity.

UNDERSTANDING TRANSGENDER

I want to tell you the story of my clients Maggie and Susan (not their real names). Maggie was born and raised as a boy named John, went to a prestigious college, became a CFO of a company, and married a woman named Janice. To the outside world, John was very successful. Inside, John was tormented, feeling like a woman trapped in the body of a man. Sometime around the age of 50, John couldn't take it any more and confessed to Janice that he needed to transition and finally become a woman. Janice was supportive and John began the expensive and painful process of transitioning genders: hormone therapy, electrolysis, assorted surgeries and more.

John became Maggie.

Sadly, Janice got sick with cancer and died, leaving Maggie alone. She then began the process of dating for the first time. Eventually she met Susan through an online dating website and they became inseparable. I was then hired to plan their wedding. Their lesbian wedding. John had changed genders and become Maggie, which then caused her sexuality to change from straight to gay.

Sound complicated? It is.

Working with Maggie and Susan was one of the most profound experiences I ever had as a wedding planner. I'll never forget shopping with Maggie for her wedding dress. She was so nervous about her hairpiece falling off and being treated poorly by the bridal salon staff. She was afraid that her shoulders were too broad and that she didn't have hips for a wedding gown. I made an appointment for us and triple-checked that our sales associate was going to be amazing. Those few hours were so powerful. Maggie looked beautiful in dress after dress. She walked out the door feeling like a million bucks and thanked me for helping her become the bride she'd always wanted to be.

The wedding day itself was also very moving. Maggie and Susan, now in their late fifties, were each escorted down the aisle of the Old South Church in Boston by their dads, men in their eighties. Both women and their dads were full of pride. What a happy ending.

That's Maggie's story and I'm grateful to be able to share that with you. Maggie wrote a book, telling some of this story herself. She is a transgender activist and educator and gives me permission to share this story, but there's a good chance that if you work with a transgender individual, you won't be privy to that kind of history. In fact, most people who are trans don't want to discuss their former name or old life prior to transition. A few additional things to note:

- If you are a wedding planner and are screening vendors and scheduling appointments for this client, tell vendors in advance that your client is transgender; even if they are comfortable with the L, G and B couples, they may not be comfortable with the T.
- It's impolite to ask about the transgender client's former name or life prior to their transition.
- When someone's gender changes, their sexuality identity may not. Just because someone may transition from F to M doesn't mean that the type of person she's attracted to also changes. Sometimes it does, but gender and sexuality are two different things.
- Some transgender people do not "pass" easily as their new gender, but you must respect the new gender regardless of their stage of transition, appearance, or voice.
- There may be extra sensitivity about family involvement or lack thereof.
- There may be a special request for gender neutral restrooms at the wedding.

FAMILY SUPPORT (OR LACK THEREOF)

Although nearly 70% of millennials support same-sex marriage, many of their parents do not. Only about two-thirds of same-sex couples have the support of both partners' parents. This can lead to lots of issues with the wedding planning. I had a groom recently who knew his dad wasn't going to be supportive but was shocked that his mom refused to participate as well. The only member of his entire family at his wedding was his younger brother. I unfortunately hear a variation of this story all the time.

These complicated family dynamics certainly affect the planning process (and this is before we even add divorce, remarriages, step-children etc. into the mix). It might be more emotional. It might be traumatic.

As you are meeting with a same-sex couple, it's only natural to want to know the nature of this dynamic. It affects the wedding and it may affect the wedding

Bad example	**Good example**
Wedding planner: How do your parents feel about all this? Couple: What do you mean? Wedding planner: Are they even chipping in or coming to the wedding? Couple: Um, both of our parents are amazing but we are paying for the wedding ourselves.	Wedding planner: Do you have the support of your parents and family? Couple: Yes, we're very lucky. Both of our parents are really awesome. I think we'll be getting a little something from them but we're not relying on them to pay for the wedding.

In the first example, the wedding planner is first assuming that the parents are not involved which is an incorrect assumption the majority of the time.

In the second example, the use of the phrase "have the support" can be interpreted in a few ways. Do they have the emotional support? The financial support? The couple can answer any way they choose.

Family dynamics can be super complicated. I have some really beautiful stories, of course, of couples who had infinite love and support from their parents and extended family, including my transgender bride, Maggie, who was escorted by her 80-something year old dad down the aisle. This is a woman who began transitioning at middle age, and it was very inspiring to see her dad's support.

On the other hand, I have a wedding coming up soon where one of the dads is attending, but not participating in family portraits, not sitting in reserved ceremony seating, not giving a toast, and otherwise, not engaging with the wedding. Why is he even coming? I'm not sure his son (my groom) can even tell me – but it is what it is, and I'll be watching him like a hawk to make sure he's not disruptive!

There are often guests similar to my groom's dad, appearing stressed or anxious to be there. Sometimes my wife works on wedding days with me, and when she does, she's often approached by such an anxious guest with a comment like, "Ugh, I can't believe I'm even here....I don't know how I feel about all this!" These are the guests who think my wife is straight and are venting to her!

WE ARE FAMILY

If you ever hear someone remark, "oh, she's definitely family" after meeting a complete stranger, chances are the person is not referring to a long-lost blood relative. Because it was very common throughout history for families to disown or repudiate their gay or lesbian sons or daughters, the LGBTQ community served as a surrogate family. This chosen family became more important during the years when many gay men were dying of AIDS and estranged from their biological families.

Fortunately in contemporary America, this is becoming less common, but it is still a sad reality for many young LGBTQ people. This idea of a second family—a family willingly chosen from friendships—has been central to the LGBTQ community. The term "family" has become code for recognizing each other in public, particularly in situations where it might not be safe to be visibly out.

GAY-THEMED

I love P!nk and I love what she said here in this statement: *I think the best day will be when we no longer talk about being gay or straight. It's not a gay wedding. It's just a wedding. It's not a gay marriage. It's just a marriage.*

There will be a day at some point when the wedding industry is fully integrated and P!nk is right! But keep in mind that some same-sex couples actually want a gay wedding. They might not want just a wedding, but rather a big GAY wedding!

They might incorporate elements of LGBT culture like drag kings or queens, go-go boys, or extremely attractive service staff. They might want readings by LGBT writers in their ceremony. They might make their ceremony political. They might want music by LGBT icons. For some couples, it's just a wedding and they simply want to be treated with kindness and respect. And some couples want this to be the GAYEST gay wedding ever!

It's our job to give it to them! Bottom line – we are in the business of customer service.

CHAPTER 3

The Laws

The obvious question is: *Why do I need to know about laws? I'm a wedding planner/caterer/etc. Why does this matter to my business?*

Well, if it matters to your clients, then it should matter to you. And believe me, laws affecting the LGBT community matter to your clients (or at least they should). Let's get started with some basic terminology and then move into the specifics.

DEFINING MARRIAGE

According to the Merriam-Webster Dictionary, the definitions of marriage are:

1. a) the state of being united to a person of the opposite sex as husband or wife in a consensual and contractual relationship recognized by law; b) the state of being united to a person of the same sex in a relationship like that of a traditional marriage; c) the mutual relation of married persons: wedlock; d) the institution whereby individuals are joined in a marriage

2. an act of marrying or the rite by which the married status is effected; especially the wedding ceremony and attendant festivities or formalities

3. an intimate or close union

The most important things to note about this definition are the presence of the word "law" and the absence of the word "religious."

Every marriage in the United States is a civil marriage because first and foremost, a marriage is a legal contract between two people that is officially recognized by the state. Many people have a religious ceremony, but without the civil marriage license, a religious marriage has no legal standing, and it is not valid in the eyes of the law. **This is the key point of misinformation regarding the fight for marriage equality.**

LGBTQ couples are not fighting for the right to be married in a Catholic or Baptist church; we are fighting for the right to obtain a legal, civil marriage license that is recognized as valid and legal by the state and the federal government. This is not about forcing a church or denomination to marry gay couples—this is about civil rights and equal treatment before the law.

Other terms you should know:

> **Civil Union:** A legal union of a same-sex couple, sanctioned by a state. This term is primarily used in the United States. Historically, civil unions have acted as litmus tests for full marriage rights. The first state to grant civil unions was Vermont, which now has full marriage equality. Other states that started with civil unions but now have full marriage include Connecticut, New Hampshire, Rhode Island and Delaware.

> **Domestic Partnership:** A legal term that refers to two cohabitating individuals; the term may (depending on the jurisdiction) bring with it certain legal protections and benefits.

> **Civil Partnership:** A legal union of a same-sex couple, sanctioned by the federal government. This provides all the benefits of marriage while using a different term. Civil partnerships originated in the United Kingdom.

> **Commitment Ceremony:** An event that celebrates a relationship, generally without any legal implications.

Based on these definitions, does a civil union mean the same thing as a marriage? Yes, it is a legal union that is sanctioned and recognized by the state. However, there are three key things to consider:

1. A civil union is a separate and unequal institution. Same-sex couples get some of the same benefits from the state as a married couple, but not all.

2. A civil union is not recognized by the federal government and provides no federal benefits.

3. Wording matters. Civil unions and marriages are unequal in rights, unequal before the law, and unequal in societal values. Would you prefer your heterosexual son or daughter to choose a civil union or a marriage?

THE STATE OF THE STATES

This map shows the marriage equality progress (or lack thereof) in the United States. Note that the world marriage equality map can be found on page 15.

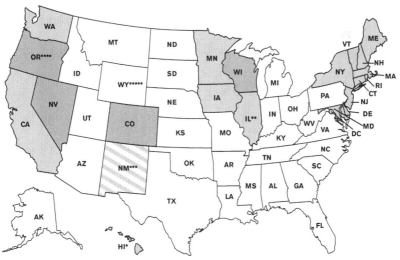

Updated November 20, 2013

States that issue marriage licenses to same-sex couples (16 states and D.C.): California (2013), Connecticut (2008), Delaware (2013), District of Columbia (2010), Hawaii* (Dec. 2013), Illinois** (June 2014) Iowa (2009), Maine (2012), Maryland, (2013), Massachusetts (2004), Minnesota (2013), New Hampshire (2010), New Jersey (2013), New York (2011), Rhode Island (2013), Vermont (2009) and Washington (2012).

States that provide the equivalent of state-level spousal rights to same-sex couples within the state (3 states and D.C.): Colorado (civil unions, 2013), District of Columbia (domestic partnerships, 2002), Nevada (domestic partnerships, 2009), and Oregon**** (domestic partnerships, 2008).

States that provide some statewide spousal rights to same-sex couples within the state (1 state): Wisconsin (domestic partnerships, 2009).

* **Hawaii:** The marriage law will go into effect on December 2, 2013.

** **Illinois:** Marriages will start taking place on June 1, 2014.

*** **New Mexico:** In Aug. 2013, at least 6 counties began issuing marriage licenses to same-sex couples pending a definitive statement of the law. In Jan. 2011, the New Mexico Attorney General issued an advisory opinion declaring that the state can recognize out-of-jurisdiction same-sex marriages. At this time, it is unclear what effect this opinion will have.

**** **Oregon:** On October 16, 2013, Oregon's Chief Operating Officer and Director of Administrative Services sent a memo to all state agencies ordering the recognition of all legal marriages performed out-of-state, including those of same-sex couples.

***** **Wyoming:** On June 6, 2011, the Wyoming Supreme Court decided *Christensen v. Christensen*, ruling that Wyoming trial courts have the ability to hear divorce proceedings terminating same-sex marriages created in other jurisdictions.

Human Rights Campaign | 1640 Rhode Island Ave., N.W., Washington, D.C. 20036 | www.hrc.org/statelaws

ANTI-DISCRIMINATION LAWS

In our study (with Community Marketing and Insights) of over 900 married and engaged same-sex couples, about 1/4 reported experiencing discrimination or heterosexism when planning their wedding. Here are some stories we heard:

We ordered our wedding invitations from a website and received a response saying that the owners were Christians who do not approve of same sex relationships. They said that they would not refuse our order, but would donate all proceeds to an ex-gay organization.

The original hotel we were going to have our reception at canceled after we went in for the tour. The hotel wedding concierge we had been working with suddenly wouldn't return our calls. Finally he told us they had booked another event on our date and couldn't host our reception. They refunded our deposit, but we had to reprint our invitations because of the change.

Every state in the United States has its own anti-discrimination policy. Those individual policies typically say things like, "you cannot discriminate on the basis of race, religion, gender..." when allowing access to things open to the public (public access). Twenty-nine of the U.S. states do not include sexual orientation or gender identity in those laws. That means that in 29 states a wedding photographer can say to you, "I'm not going to photograph your wedding because you're gay." And it's perfectly legal.

As a wedding professional, it's your job to make sure that never happens to your LGBT clients. But we'll come back to that later. For now, take note of the states that prohibit discrimination:

Anti-Discrimination Laws That Include Sexual Orientation and Gender Identity

- Minnesota
- Rhode Island
- New Mexico
- California
- District of Columbia
- Illinois
- Maine
- Hawaii
- New Jersey
- Washington
- Iowa
- Oregon
- Vermont
- Colorado

Anti-Discrimination Laws That Only Include Sexual Orientation

- Wisconsin
- Massachusetts
- Connecticut
- New Hampshire
- Nevada
- Maryland
- New York
- Delaware

State Nondiscrimination Laws in the U.S.
This map was last updated on June 21, 2013

States banning discrimination based on sexual orientation and gender identity/expression (17 states and the District of Columbia)
Minnesota (1993); Rhode Island (1995, 2001)[1]; New Mexico (2003); California (1992, 2003)[1]; District of Columbia (1977, 2005)[1]; Illinois (2005); Maine (2005); Hawaii (1991, 2005, 2006, 2011)[2]; New Jersey (1992, 2006)[1]; Washington (2006); Iowa (2007); Oregon (2007); Vermont (1992, 2007)[1]; Colorado (2007); Connecticut (1991, 2011)[1]; Nevada (1999, 2011)[1]; Massachusetts (1989, 2011)[1]; Delaware (2009, 2013)[1]

Laws banning discrimination based on sexual orientation (4 states)
Wisconsin (1982); New Hampshire (1997); Maryland (2001); New York (2002)

[1]California, Connecticut, Delaware, DC, New Jersey, Massachusetts, Nevada, Rhode Island and Vermont first passed sexual orientation nondiscrimination laws, then later passed gender identity/expression laws

[2]In 1991, Hawaii enacted a law prohibiting sexual orientation discrimination in employment. In 2005, it enacted a law prohibiting sexual orientation and gender identity/expression discrimination in housing. In 2006, public accommodations protections were added for sexual orientation and gender identity/expression. In 2011, gender identity was added to the employment discrimination law.

National Gay and Lesbian Task Force
www.theTaskForce.org

It is illegal to discriminate on the basis of sexual orientation in all of Canada and Mexico. Mexico also prohibits gender identity discrimination, which is not explicitly stated in Canadian law but generally assumed to be the case.
The Defense of Marriage Act

The Defense of Marriage Act (DOMA) is a law that was signed by President Clinton in 1996. This law has two parts designed to discriminate against same-sex marriages:

1. The U.S. federal government does not recognize same-sex marriage and does not provide any benefits to married same-sex couples.

2. A state where gay marriage is not legal does not have to recognize a gay marriage performed in a state in which it is legal.

In June 2013, the federal portion of DOMA was overturned by the U.S. Supreme Court. The plaintiff in the case, Edie Windsor, was a married lesbian from New York who was left with a $363,000 federal estate tax bill when her wife died after 40 years together. She was forced to sell off property and drain her bank accounts to pay the taxes. If Edie's spouse had been a man, she wouldn't have owed any taxes.

Jen and I with Edie Windsor

Now, the good news is that that part of DOMA is history. The bad news is that states can still discriminate. A same-sex couple from Texas who marry in New York will not be legally married when they return to Texas, nor will they get the full range of federal benefits. See, most federal marriage benefits only apply to couples who live in states where their marriage is also legal.

However, if you are working with same-sex couples who lives in New York and wants to marry in New York, those couple will now get all the benefits of marriage.

This stuff affects me personally. When Jen and I married, we went to an estate planning attorney who specialized in LGBT issues and had all this extra paperwork drawn up – documents such as Durable Powers of Attorney, Health Care Proxies and more – that specifically identify each other as legal proxies in case one of us is injured or ill. This paperwork isn't necessary when we are in a state where our marriage is legal, but it is when we travel to a state (such as Pennsylvania and Virginia) where it's not.

If we were traveling without that paperwork and were in a car accident, we would be seen as strangers by hospital staff. This is a situation every same-sex couple wants to avoid.

Additionally, remember that cute photo of my son Patrick? Well, even though he was born to Jen, my name was on his birth certificate since he was born in Massachusetts. But to a state like Ohio, that means nothing, so I had to go to court to adopt him (and pay $2000 in legal fees), just to prove he's my son when we travel. His birth certificate with my name is meaningless in states like Ohio, but the adoption decree is the proof they need. This process is called second parent adoption, and by the way, many states don't even offer it.

I realize this is confusing and complicated. Don't blame me; blame the feds! But since laws are constantly changing (hopefully for the better), if you live in the United States, you can find the latest, updated LGBT public policy information at LGBTMap.org.

WHY DOES THIS MATTER?

In the wedding industry, we are in the business of making dreams come true, which involves a great deal of customer service. Many of us are practically therapists for our clients! If these laws affect our clients and provide extra stress, then these laws affect our wedding planning.

I give all the couples I meet with a list of professionals outside the wedding industry who can help them navigate these complicated legal waters. There are many professionals such as estate planning attorneys, financial planners, and accountants with LGBT specialties. These professionals are great resources not only for you but also for your clients.

To identify some of these professionals in your area, start with Google. If you strike out there, then look for a local chapter of the National Gay and Lesbian Chamber of Commerce (NGLCC) in your area and I'm sure you'll find some of the people I described.

Having such a list at your disposal will show your LGBT clients that you have thought beyond just their wedding day and really care about their family's protection.

CHAPTER 3 ACTION STEPS

☐ Find out how many same-sex couples there are in your state (hint: check the Williams Institute or LGBTMap.org)
☐ Find out what your state's non-discrimination policy says
☐ Find out about pending legislation or court cases in your service area
☐ Identify a marriage equality organization in your service area
☐ Identify private legal resources/family law providers/estate planning attorneys who can draw up paperwork to help same-sex couples protect their families.

Examples of paperwork include Durable Power of Attorney and Health Care Proxies.

CHAPTER 4

Your Own Company

The bottom line is this: if you value the diversity in your clients, then you must also value the diversity in your workplace. The LGBT community notices and they care about your business policies.

According to Community Marketing, Inc. about two-thirds (65%) of all LGBT adults reported that they would be very or somewhat likely to remain loyal to a brand they believed to be very friendly and supportive to the gay, lesbian and transgender community – even when less friendly companies may offer lower prices or be more convenient.

70-80% of gays and lesbians report that their purchasing decisions are favorably influenced by corporate sponsorship of LGBT (lesbian, gay, bisexual and transgender) events and participation in LGBT charities.

In fact, this is so important that the Human Rights Campaign (HRC) publishes an annual Corporate Equality Index which analyses corporations based on their policies towards their LGBT employees and customers. The Equality Index is used to create a Buying Guide (there's even an app) so LGBT consumers know which corporations to support. I know that I use the Buying Guide when making my purchasing decisions.

Find out more about the Corporate Equality Index at www.hrc.org.

CULTURAL COMPETENCY

In the workplace, we define the ability to activate a set of behaviors, practices, attitudes, and policies that enable effective, mutually beneficial work and success in cross-cultural situations as cultural competency. Cultural competency is a continuum of practices, and each organization and individual slides back and forth on the scale, depending on the situation and circumstances.

There are six levels:

- Cultural Destructiveness: forced assimilation, subjugation, rights and privileges for dominant groups only
- Cultural Incapacity: racism, stereotypes, unfair hiring practices
- Cultural Blindness: differences ignored, normative assumptions, treating everyone as sharing the same culture, only meeting needs of dominant groups
- Cultural Pre-Competence: exploring cultural issues, assessing needs of organization and individuals
- Cultural Competence: recognizing individual and cultural differences, seeking advice from diverse groups, valuing diversity within and outside the organization
- Cultural Proficiency: implementing changes to improve services based upon cultural needs, approaching interpersonal and professional interactions with cultural respect and openness, always attending to language, employing marketing and policy usages that indicate diversity

HOW TO MOVE BEYOND GOOD INTENTIONS AND MAKE REAL CHANGE

We all roll our eyes at the "all talk/no action" type of person who pays lip service to equal rights but makes not effort to change his or her behavior . How can you take your lists about the value of diversity and turn them into real, actionable strategies? Here are five general strategies to implement. In later units, we will develop a more specific action plan for your business needs.

1. If you do not have one in place, create a non-discrimination policy for your company that includes sexual orientation and gender identity.
A non-discrimination policy that is incorporated into both the HR policies and the core values of your company is essential. You can even include the policy on your website. Here is an example:

We are committed to creating a culture that reflects the diversity of our clients. With that goal in mind, we encourage our employees to understand, accept, and celebrate differences among people. We welcome everyone and prohibit all discrimination on the basis of race, ethnicity, age, religion, physical ability, sexual orientation, gender identity and gender.

2. Reexamine your everyday and professional language use.
Never underestimate the power of first impressions or pronoun and gender-specific labels on forms. If a staff member takes a call from a bride, will the staff member automatically ask for the groom's name? Do your forms have labels for bride and groom instead of spouse one and two? In the break-room, do staff members joke around and use phrases like "that's so gay!" or "that's so lame!"? Do you find yourself more comfortable or at ease with clients or customers who look or act like you? Can you accommodate bilingual or multilingual speakers?

3. Take HR policies seriously and evaluate whether they discriminate against particular groups or create hardships for others.
Insurance is the buzzword these days—do you have fair policies on spousal, family, and domestic partner additions? Do you have a policy about parental leave instead of maternal leave? Are there ways to make the workplace more flexible to accommodate child-rearing or elder-caretaking?

4. Create a no-tolerance policy for political, racist, sexist, sizeist, ableist, xenophobic, etc. email forwards.
Humor is wonderful and often walks the line between edgy and controversial. But in the workplace, never ever assume that your coworkers share your politics or your humor. One person's edgy humor is another person's humiliating and infuriating stereotype. When these types of emails are forwarded through an office, they shut down the very doors of dialogue and workplace cohesion

you are trying to open.

5. Institute a monthly diversity discussion group where employees can troubleshoot, share, and get support around challenging diversity issues in the workplace or with clients.

An atmosphere where everyone is too afraid to speak because they don't want to be politically incorrect is just as counterproductive as the other extreme. Honest dialogue and real questions are necessary for this process to be successful. If a staff member feels awkward around gay clients, shaming her is not going to fix the problem. But if she can bring her feelings up in a supportive professional environment and her colleagues can offer suggestions or new perspectives, then the employee will learn and develop more effective ways of handling, and even discarding, these feelings.

CHAPTER 4 ACTION STEPS

☐ Find out how to add sexual orientation and gender identity to your corporate anti-discrimination policy if it's not already there.

Sample:

We are committed to creating a culture that reflects the diversity of our clients. With that goal in mind, we encourage our employees to understand, accept, and celebrate differences among people. We welcome everyone and prohibit all discrimination on the basis of race, ethnicity, age, religion, physical ability, sexual orientation, gender identity and gender.

☐ Assess your staff. Are all of your staff members open and affirming of same-sex couples and LGBT individuals?

☐ Does your HR training include any diversity training that specifically includes LGBT issues? What about LGBT wedding issues?

☐ Does your Sales and Marketing training include any diversity training that specifically includes LGBT issues? What about LGBT wedding issues?

CHAPTER 5

Data and Travel Trends

Here's some food for thought – check out these fascinating, random facts about the varied LGBT community and wedding market:

- There are 646,000 same-sex couples living together in the U.S., according to the latest Census. 131,000 reported being "married," but that term is subjective.

- In the 2011 Canadian census, there were 21,015 legally married couples. Two-thirdsof gay and lesbian couples (approximately 43,560) in Canada are unmarried. Just under half of all same-sex couples lived in Toronto (21%), Montréal (18%), and Vancouver (10%).

- The INEGI in Mexico that collects Census data doesn't track this gay and lesbian data.

- In June 2006, Forbes estimated that if same-sex marriage was legalized nationwide, gay marriages could potentially boost the overall wedding industry by $9.5 billion per year.

- There are about 7 million LGBT people in the United

- Nationwide, gay and lesbian buying power has been estimated at $790 billion as of 2013.

- There are about 7 million LGBT people in the United States (who have come out on surveys).

- About 4-5% of the population is gay or lesbian; about 7% are LGBT.

- There have been approximately 110,000 legal gay marriages in the United States since 2004 and another 50,000 around the world, according to the Williams Institute. Of these marriages, 66% are two women, except in New York.

- An estimated 19% of LGBT-identified adults have a child under 18 in their home right now.

- A new study indicates that 48% of gays and lesbians keep up on the latest trends compared to 38% of their heterosexual counterparts.

- 53% of gay men vs. 30% of straight men keep up with the latest consumer trends and be early adopters of products.

- 45% of gays and lesbians are likely to upgrade to the latest model of a product, compared to 33% of straight men and women.

- More than half (54%) of gay men and lesbian respondents report reading some type of blog as of June 2010, compared to only 40% of heterosexuals.

Source: Harris Interactive

SUPPORT FOR SAME-SEX MARRIAGE

Support for same-sex marriage has rapidly accelerated over the past 10 years, and now more Americans support same-sex marriage rights than oppose it. In a variety of recent surveys, the support level is at an average of 53%, up from an average of 33% in 2004, back when it became legal in Massachusetts.

Not surprisingly, the Millennial generation largely supports same-sex marriage, which is actually good news for your business in terms of marketing. When your straight wedding clients support same-sex marriage, then you should worry less about including some mention of marriage equality or gay weddings on your own website. If your straight clients aren't turned off by it, then you can only benefit by being fully inclusive.

Millennials' Support for Same-Sex Marriage

Country	%
Netherlands	83%
Spain	81%
Sweden	81%
Germany	78%
Canada	78%
Argentina	78%
Italy	74%
United Kingdom	74%
France	71%
Mexico	70%
Australia	69%
United States	68%
Greece	66%
Japan	64%
China	62%
Brazil	60%
South Africa	55%
Poland	54%
Singapore	52%
India	49%
Turkey	46%
Russia	39%

VIMNinsights.tumblr.com
@VIMNinsights

THE NEXT NORMAL

Credit: Viacom International Media Networks

CASE STUDY: NEW YORK CITY

When same-sex marriage became legal in New York state in 2011, the projected financial benefit was about $100 million per year. Nobody expected New York City alone to benefit by $259 million in the very first year of same-sex marriage. Here are some of the astounding facts and figures from year one of same-sex marriage in New York City:

- 201,600 guests visited from outside the five boroughs
- 94,400 guests came from within the five boroughs
- 235,000 total hotel rooms were rented, at a daily rate of $275 per room – that's $64,625,000 to the hotel industry alone, not counting food and beverage!
- 31% of couples spent $10,000 or more.
- The average spent was $9,039 per wedding celebration – which is fairly high considering all of the City Hall weddings.
- There were about 8,200 marriage licenses issued that first year
- 47.5% of those couples marrying were two guys; 40% were too women; and 12% didn't were same-sex couples not identifying as specifically gay or lesbian.

There are so many notable things to extract from this data. For example, I think it's very interesting that 12% of the same-sex couples who married didn't identify as gay or lesbian – that implies that they feel somewhere in the middle AKA queer (though please don't use that word!)

WHAT HAPPENS WHEN LGBT COUPLES TRAVEL OUT OF STATE TO GET LEGALLY MARRIED

Within a single week, my company helped five same-sex couples from other states (Nevada, California, Pennsylvania, Mississippi, and Texas) legally marry in Massachusetts. This "elopement" service simply guides and manages out-of-state couples through the process of making their marriage legal. Last year we worked with fifty-three couples from twenty-seven states. This service brings a lot of money into my company and into the state of Massachusetts.

At least half of these out-of-state couples plan a party or a celebration and/or a marriage reenactment when they return home. If you don't work in a state where gay marriage is legal, you may still get business from these couples. If you answer your phone and speak to a man who is inquiring about a wedding celebration, are you going to ask him the name of his bride? Be careful. It's just that type of assumption that can cost you business.

Gay and lesbian couples from all over the United States are traveling to legally marry and then planning a party back home. These parties require vendors from the wedding and hospitality industry. You may need to be ready sooner than you think.

You don't have to wait until gay marriage is legal in your state. By creating relationships with your existing clientele, repositioning your marketing materials, and revving up the word-of-mouth referrals within the LGBTQ community, your business will be in the perfect position to capture the rush of same-sex weddings when it does happen. In the meantime, you will reap the benefits of cultivating a new customer base.

LGBT-FRIENDLY DESTINATION WEDDING LOCATIONS

The business of gay destination weddings is starting to emerge although the LGBT population has been traveling widely for a long time. In addition to the countries where same-sex marriage is legal, the following is a list of top countries for gay honeymoons and destination weddings/commitment ceremonies:

- Mexico
- The U.S. Virgin Islands
- Puerto Rico
- Costa Rica
- Curacao

- Australia
- New Zealand
- United Kingdom
- France
- Spain

But where are we going on vacation? Community Marketing Inc. did a study and these are the findings:

Top Travel Leisure Destinations – Canadian LGBTs		**Top International Travel Leisure Destination – U.S. LGBTS**	
Destination	% Visited	Destination	% Visited
Montreal	25%	Canada	13%
Toronto	25%	England	9%
Vancouver	17%	France	8%
New York City, NY	16%	Mexico	8%
Seattle	12%	Spain	7%
Calgary	12%	Germany	6%
Las Vegas, NV	11%	Italy	6%
Ottawa	11%	Montreal, Canada	5%
San Francisco, CA	11%	Toronto, Canada	5%
Banff	9%	Vancouver, Canada	5%
England	8%	Australia	4%
Quebec City	8%	Netherlands	4%
Victoria	8%	Puerto Vallarta, Mexico	4%
Whistler	8%	Cancun, Mexico	3%
L.A./W. Hollywood, CA	7%		
Halifax	7%		

Gay Men: 2012 Leisure Destination Among Gay Men in the U.S.

Destination	%Visited
New York City, NY	24%
San Francisco, CA	19%
Chicago, IL	17%
Las Vegas, NV	17%
L.A./W. Hollywood, CA	15%
Washington, DC	14%
Ft. Lauderdale/ Wilton Manors. FL	13%
Palm Springs, CA	11%
Orlando, FL	10%
San Diego, CA	10%
Boston, MA	10%
Miami/South Beach, FL	10%
New Orleans, LA	9%
Atlanta, GA	7%
Denver, CO	7%

Lesbians: 2012 Leisure Destination Among Lesbians in the U.S.

Destination	%Visited
New York City, NY	16%
San Francisco, CA	15%
Las Vegas, NV	13%
Chicago, IL	12%
Washington, DC	11%
L.A /Hollywood,CA	10%
Boston, MA	9%
San Diego, CA	9%
Orlando, FL	8%
Atlanta, GA	7%
Seattle, WA	7%
Hawaii	7%
Provincetown, MA	7%
Portland, OR	7%

See, we are only 5% of the adult population, but we take twice as many trips as the average American.

Lesbians travel more to Mexico.

Gay men travel more to Europe.

American gay and lesbian tourists expected to spend an average of $2,300 for vacations during the spring and summer, whereas heterosexual travelers planned to spend $1,500 for the same period, according to Harris Interactive.

Philadelphia did a big marketing campaign to attract gay and lesbian tourists. The theme was "Get Your History Straight and Your Nightlife Gay." The campaign was widely considered a success. The city reported that every $1 spent on their marketing effort generated $153 in visitor spending, and gay overnight visitors spent twice as much as general overnight visitors.

In short, LGBT travel is BIG business as more and more destinations around the world offer legal same-sex marriage, and destination weddings are going to be huge!

CHAPTER 6

Let's Talk About Weddings

WHAT'S THE DIFFERENCE BETWEEN A STRAIGHT WEDDING AND A GAY WEDDING?

This question is one of the most common questions I get.
The answer is: a lot. And also — not very much at all.

I hear *"Love is love!"* all the time. But in the eyes of many family members and politicians, love is not love. This makes planning a gay wedding much more complicated. For example, almost all of my clients have some family members (often parents) who don't accept the marriage and won't attend the wedding. It's very emotional when one of my brides tells me about her dad who won't attend the wedding. Or the groom whose mom won't dance with him — and actually, would rather not be there.

And as you learned in Chapter 3, in 29 U.S. states, it's legal to refuse services to a couple just because they're LGBT. Those are states where a wedding pho-tographer could literally say to a couple, *"I won't shoot your wedding because you're gay."* Could you imagine hearing that when planning your own wedding? It's not fun, but it's the reality that same-sex couples face. They essentially have to come out of the closet over and over again.

And then there's the matter of walking down the aisle. Who goes last? What if there are no brides? Or two brides? Well, we work it all out — often with two aisles — so each partner gets his or her moment (and I get another place to decorate).

So yes, the wedding planning is different for same-sex couples. But the weddings themselves? They look pretty similar, actually — but they feel much different.

Same-sex weddings usually have a ceremony, cocktail hour, then dinner and dancing. Everyone sits at tables and has a nice dinner. There are toasts and sometimes a cake cutting, but the cake topper won't be one bride and one groom. Pretty predictable stuff. But gay weddings are often not religious or traditional and frequently don't have events like receiving lines or garter tosses. Sometimes there are no wedding party members, and often the dad doesn't walk his daughter down the aisle.

But the love is there in abundance. In the hundreds of legal weddings in which I've been a part, there is an amazing sense of equality and spirit of triumph. The energy is exhilarating. I've had clients in their eighties, together for 40 years, and these couples can finally get married. The weddings celebrate that achievement, and do not take it for granted.

It pays to be flexible.

Whether you are a wedding planner, catering manager, florist, or hotel manager, when you work with LGBT wedding clients, you will need to check your industry assumptions at the door and be willing to be creative, flexible, and open. This training will give you a set of tools and information to use as guides, but most importantly, you should cultivate your professional mindset to think outside the typical wedding box.

While we have heard of extremely conservative and traditional gay weddings, they happen very rarely. Think about it this way: most heterosexual couples start planning their wedding with a nearly complete script about how it is "supposed" to look. This script comes from religion, families, ethnic culture, and Hollywood. Even the most DIY opposite-sex couples reference this script by rebelling against it. But in a world where same-sex marriage is still mostly illegal, who writes the script? The couples and their communities do. Imagine the freedom that comes with being able to write the screenplay of your own wedding day. Parents and grandparents may never have been to a gay wedding before—so they are hard-pressed to come up with any expectations at all!

Yes, as we've shared above, there are gay wedding traditions. And yes, many same-sex couples will choose many of the traditional elements of straight weddings. But as a wedding industry professional, imagine not having a script. Of course, you have to retain your professional judgment about things that work and things that don't. Because we are in the wedding industry, we tend to forget the real meanings of the symbols and traditions included in the general wedding script. Sometimes these meanings are beautiful and inspiring, but sometimes they can be constricting and narrow.

Coming Out

Do you know what it means to "come out of the closet"?

Coming out is something that LGBT people have to do on an ongoing basis. They have to first come out to themselves, then family, friends, co-workers, neighbors and on and on. And when it comes to planning their wedding, they have to keep coming out again and again – to the vendors they hire and the vendors they don't. Every time they call or inquire about a wedding venue, an officiant, or a photographer, the issue of sexual orientation arises.

And as we learned earlier in this chapter, in some U.S. states, wedding professionals can legally say, "No, I don't want to work with you because you are gay."

The average wedding involves 43 different vendors. These include the venue, the valet, the jeweler, the florist and much more. A same-sex couple may literally have to come out 100 or more times while planning their wedding. That's nuts!

But that's where you come in. When you are working with same-sex couples, it's going to be your job to come out for them. After they meet and hire you, they should never have to come out again because you'll be referring them to trusted, LGBT-friendly and inclusive professionals. It'll be your job to protect your clients from discriminatory laws.

Privacy Concerns

The first thing you should know is that you may have some couples who are very concerned about their privacy. For example, they may not be fully out of the closet in the workplace. Or they may have a high profile job where their sexuality needs to be more discreet. Or they may not be out to family members. You must respect each individual's request for privacy. You may be told specifically not to use their wedding photos for promotion on your website or in your portfolio. Or, you may be told that you can only use photos with no identifying details.

I know this is painful, at times, particularly when we've worked so hard on a project, but we must respect each individual's right to privacy. In my first few years in business (back in 2004-2005), when even fewer people were out, I was lucky to have any photos at all to show to prospective clients. I was asked time and time again to keep photos private. It was frustrating but I understood. I've had numerous couples strike out or amend the "image use" clause in my contract.

I know some wedding photographers may ask to charge a couple extra money if they don't have permission to use the wedding photos. After all, the photographer is giving up a right – I understand but I still don't think it's cool.

The Proposal: Who Gets the Ring?

One of the cool things about gay weddings is that there is frequently two of everything. Two dresses or two tuxes. Two aisles. And yes, often two proposals and two engagement rings.

Think about it — in a straight wedding, the guy saves up three months of his salary (thank you, Diamond Industry!) to buy an engagement ring. He may hire a Proposal Planner to craft the perfect engagement experience. He gets down on one knee, and well, you know the rest.

With gay weddings, anything goes. And I've heard it all.

Most of my clients have been together 10 or more years so they typically already wear rings. Their proposals may be highly unromantic and go something like this:

"Hey, now that it's legal to marry in New York, we should probably get married."
"Are you asking me to marry you?"
"I guess so."
"Sure, let's do it. We should really find a great gay wedding planner."

The legalization of same-sex marriage in a new state prompts a flurry of proposals — and most of them are not what you'd expect from a traditional wedding.

Still, there is plenty of room for creativity. I love that same-sex couples who do have a proper "pop the question" type experience often get to experience it twice. See, most couples end up taking turns. If one partner is surprised, then the other partner is often surprised at a later date. And usually the answer is still an enthusiastic "YES"!

The surprises are varied. I've had proposals out of Scrabble pieces, artwork, Trivial Pursuit cards, and on top of the Space Needle. The same type of creativity that comes with straight engagements certainly applies here — but twice!

What about the rings? Rosie O'Donnell bought her now wife Michelle Rounds a big diamond engagement ring. Is that the expectation? It's not a clear-cut answer.

Same-sex couples (both male and female) who unromantically propose now that it's legal probably already have rings. In this case, they will often buy wedding bands to substitute for their existing rings, skipping over engagement rings all together.

Some brides like Michelle (and my wife) get the big diamond engagement ring at their proposal. Some brides get cufflinks, a necklace or (like me) a beautiful, non-diamond engagement ring. Most grooms, however, stick with the one ring, and their proposal happens without an engagement ring — though I've had a few sets of grooms who want the big diamond, but in their wedding band instead.

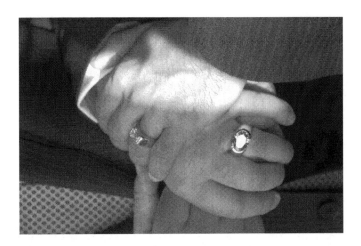

Showers and Parties

Of course wedding showers and bachelor and bachelorette parties are heterosexual traditions but they're also a really good time—and another excuse for a party. Your gay and lesbian clients may ask you about how these work for same-sex couples.

Same-sex couples who are more settled tend not to have these parties, while couples that are starting out (and of typical marrying age) often do. And these parties are generally open to all genders!

The gay men have wedding showers, too - they are not reserved for just the brides. Showers are joint operations, with both partners in attendance. Although some gay men call it a "thunderstorm" not a shower – how masculine!

When it comes to the bachelor/bachelorette parties, some same-sex couples have a joint party and some have separate parties. If they have separate groups of friends, separate parties are generally the way to go. But if their friends are merged, then I suggest a big party. I have two brides who are partying independently and meeting up at a club at the end of the night.

Real Wedding Case Study #1: Carlos and Andrew

Carlos and Andrew married in New Hampshire. They wanted to be married in an Episcopal church. At that time, Episcopal churches only married same-sex couples in one place in the United States: Eastern Massachusetts. So the grooms had to find another officiant and had a secular ceremony.

One of the grooms "came out" to his family via his wedding invitation. Some family members had previously not known he was gay.

These grooms wanted to run a wedding announcement in the local paper and were denied because the paper (The New Hampshire Union Leader) didn't run same-sex wedding announcements.

Real Wedding Case Study #2: Bill and Nick

One of the grooms had agreed to father children with a lesbian couple and has two teenage children now. They were very young when he met his partner. Because of DOMA and tax rules (they lived in Texas), he married one of the lesbians. He had to get a divorce from the lesbian before his wedding so he could then marry his partner.

At their wedding, the lesbian couple, the two grooms, and the teenage kids (who go back and forth between families) were in attendance. The grooms had professional hair & makeup artist on site for them. Bill and Nick were married by a former priest.

Again: one wedding and lots of unique elements.

COMPARING WEDDINGS

I find that people understand the differences most easily when I compare the most traditional of straight weddings to the most nontraditional of gay weddings. It helps to visualize, blow-by-blow, all the tiny differences; they do add up! I'm giving a quick rundown here but you can read about these differences more in-depth in Chapters 7 and 8.

At a Straight Wedding

Don't have to call and ask "do you work with straight couples?

Use the tradition, "Something old, something new, something borrowed, something blue"

1/3 of marriage ceremonies are in a place of worship

The couple gets dressed and ready for the wedding separately

There is often a break between the ceremony and the reception for photos and travel time between venues.

The guests know what to expect because, chances are, they have been to many straight weddings before.

Most weddings don't have pre-ceremony drinks available to the guests, besides occasionally water.

The processional is often the Bridal March or a similar classical tune.

The bride wears a veil and a dress.

There is often a receiving line

The seating has a bride's side & a groom's side

At a Gay Wedding

Have to call and come out by asking "Do you work with gay couples?"

We almost never use the "Something old, something new, something borrowed, something blue" tradition.

93% of gay men and 77% of lesbians get dressed and ready for the wedding together

78% of gay men and 59% of lesbians enter together holding hands. One-third of lesbians walk down two separate aisles or from two different directions.

There is typically no break after the ceremony— we start the party right away!

The guests don't know what to expect because most guests are straight and have never been to a gay wedding. This is an opportunity for us to really have fun with the plans!

There is often champagne or a signature cocktail served before the ceremony (or even a full bar)

81% of gay men enter together holding hands. One-third of lesbians walk down two separate aisles or from two different directions.

At a Straight Wedding (cont.)	At a Gay Wedding (cont.)
There are often big bridal parties	The processional is often a pop tune or if classical, seldom the Bridal March.
The ceremony is not political	
Formal photos are often taken during cocktail hour	We seldom have veils and 12% of lesbian couples have neither partner in a dress.
There is often a guestbook	
The bride's parents often pay for all or part of the wedding	There is almost never a receiving line
	Free seating for all is most common
Parents invite colleagues, neighbors and old friends	The bridal party is usually very small and may not be called a bridal party; 36% have no attendants
The size of the wedding averages 150+ guests	The ceremony is political with usually some reference to marriage equality, or a reading regarding marriage equality.
Involved Mother of the Bride/Groom (MOB)	
	Formal photos are most often taken before the ceremony
	The guests often sign a Foundation Covenant sacred text/sign-in board to capture the joy and validation received from guests as frameable art.
	67% of same-sex couples pay for the wedding themselves
	The size of the wedding averages 75-100 guests, and many are smaller than that
	MOB very seldom involved

THE WEDDING PARTY

When you are working with a same-sex couple, don't forget that about one-third of those couples have no one standing up with them at all. And if they do, they are probably not called the "bridal party" – as we now know, "bridal" is a very heterosexist word! I personally use the term attendants to refer to the wedding party because it's a nice and gender-neutral term that avoids misunderstandings.

But you may have some very creative same-sex couples who choose to use any of the following (or something else entirely!) Remember, I don't make this stuff up!

- Attendants
- Honor Attendants
- Team *insert couple name here*
- Best People/Person
- Bridesmates
- Bridesmen
- Bridesguys
- Bridespeeps
- Bridal Brigade
- Wonder Women
- Bridespeople
- Groomspeeps
- Groomspeople

Keep in mind that the bridesmates may be male or female, or genderqueer – or whatever! They may be wearing a suit, a dress or something else.

Let's do a quick demonstration on how to have this conversation with your client or a prospective client to minimize awkwardness and apologies:

Bad example

Wedding planner: How large is your bridal party?
Couple: One woman on each side, um, but we're not brides.
Wedding planner: Sorry! Your wedding party... are you going to pick out their dresses for them?
Couple: Um, one of them is in a suit!

Good example

Wedding planner: Are you planning to have any attendants?
Couple: Yes, one woman on each side.
Wedding planner: What are they going to wear?
Couple: One will wear a dress and one will wear a suit.

Note the use of open-ended questions to get the information you need. No assumptions are made. It's easy!

THE GAY WEDDING INVITATION

Is there such a thing as a gay wedding invitation? Shouldn't invitations be the same for straight and gay couples? As with everything else, there are subtle changes. First of all, remember that most same-sex couples are paying for the wedding themselves. This often means that the names of parents are not on the invitation, inviting the guests to the wedding. Here are two examples:

Traditional with one set of parents hosting:
Mr. and Mrs. John L. Smith
request the honor of your presence
at the marriage of their daughter
Mary Ann
and
Edward Malcolm Jones

More common with same-sex couples:
Eliza May Jones
and
Mary Ann Smith
request the honor of your presence

GAY-THEMED INVITATIONS

As a wedding planner, many businesses reach out to me, asking for referrals and for me to promote their products to my clients and other same-sex couples. One product I am frequently asked about is invitations for same-sex weddings.

Quite simply, just because it's a gay wedding doesn't mean it's a gay-themed wedding. If we are having a beach ceremony, well then the invitation may have seashells and waves, not rainbow flags. If we are having a wedding in a barn, then the invitation may have some rustic imagery, not two women's symbols. I think you get the picture, but many businesses do not. Google "gay wedding invitations" to see what I mean.

If you think it's cheesy, your clients probably do, too.

A design that reflects the theme of the wedding is more common

FORMAL ADDRESSING

It's confusing to figure out how to address invitations to LGBT couples. Here's the rundown on how envelopes are addressed:

---

1) Outer envelope: If they are an unmarried couple, the names should be alphabetized and set on two separate lines, for example:

Ms. Jennifer Coveney
Ms. Bernadette Smith
14 Willow Street
Boston, MA
02110

Inner envelope: *Ms. Coveney and Ms. Smith*

---

2) Outer envelope: If they are married with different last names, the names should be alphabetized and set on the same line, for example:

Ms. Jennifer Coveney and Ms. Bernadette Smith
14 Willow Street
Boston, MA
02110

Inner envelope: *Ms. Coveney and Ms. Smith*

3) Outer envelope: If they are married with the same last name, the names should be alphabetized and set on the same line, for example:

Mrs. and Mrs. Bernadette and Jennifer Coveney-Smith
14 Willow Street
Boston, MA
02110

Inner envelope: *Mrs. and Mrs. Coveney-Smith*

P.S. That's not our real address!

REGISTRIES (BESIDES THE OBVIOUS)

Where do same-sex couples register for wedding gifts? What's normal for them? You'll find that many gay and lesbian couples have already been together for years, accumulating a houseful of great stuff —and just don't need to register. Many others would rather have their guests support an important charity instead of spending money on gifts (or wedding favors, for that matter).

But as with everything else, this is an individual decision but let's run through the options:

Major registry: This could be a Bloomingdale's, Crate and Barrel, Williams-Sonoma or another big store. This will always be the default option and those couples who are having a wedding shower are most likely to register at a place like this. Keep in mind that the registry form often asks one partner to be the "Bride" and the other to be the "Groom" and a partner may find him or herself on a mailing list depending on which one you pick!

Charity registry: HRC and Marriage Equality USA are two of the LGBT charities that allow couples to create their own mini webpage and allow your guests to make a direct, online donation. Those organizations will then send the couple a list of all the donors to be thanked appropriately. There are other organizations which offer this service but these are the most popular.

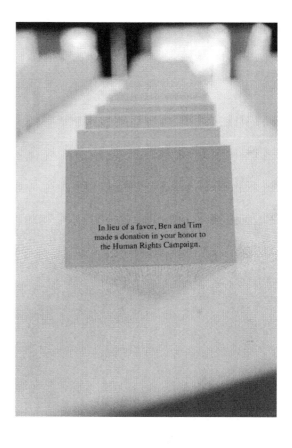

In lieu of a favor, Ben and Tim made a donation in your honor to the Human Rights Campaign.

Alternative registry: Newlywish.com is one example of an alternative registry that allows couples to register for gifts from small businesses and for gifts that are experiences, such as Broadway shows. Newlywish offers beautifully curated, thoughtfully designed products.

Honeymoon registry: Honeyfund and the like are always popular with couples (straight and gay) who already have loads of "stuff"!

DRESSING THE BRIDE, BRIDEGROOM AND GROOM

Grooms

Here are some of the many wardrobe combinations I've seen in gay grooms:

- Two grooms in morning suits
- Two grooms in tuxedos
- Two grooms in suits
- One groom in a suit and one in a tartan
- Two grooms in a shirt and tie

Most of my grooms buy their garments, although some grooms do rent their suits. For those who opt to buy, I generally send them to a made to measure tailor such as Suit Supply or Indochino. One thing is clear: it's relatively easy for a groom to buy a tuxedo without coming out of the closet, but you should still be prepared to help.

Here are a few tips for helping your gay grooms:

- Don't assume that they will wear one of the options stated above. You may encounter the occasional groom who will wear drag. Instead, ask, "What are you wearing to your wedding?" If the answer is "a dress," don't act shocked or surprised.
- Identify gay-friendly or gay-owned tailors in your area.
- Identify gay-friendly or gay-owned tuxedo rental shops in your area.

Brides

You'd think after years as a gay wedding planner, I'd have all the answers on this subject. I can tell you that for lesbian brides, figuring out what to wear is one of the greatest wedding-planning stressors. In addition, most of the lesbian brides I've worked with want something ready-to-wear, not custom made.

Here's what I've observed:
- Two brides in black cocktail dresses
- Two brides in white wedding gowns
- Two brides in white suits
- Two brides in black suits
- Brides in two dresses that match their wedding colors
- One bride in a white gown and her partner in a black suit/tuxedo
- One bride in a white gown and her partner in a white/off-white suit/tuxedo

To quantify that a bit further based on our experiences, we've seen 36% of lesbian couples wear one dress and one pantsuit or tuxedo, 27% of lesbian couples both wear a wedding gown (two gowns), and 8% of lesbian couples each wear a pants suit (two suits or tuxedos).

This also means that nearly 60% of lesbian couples are requiring at least one pantsuit. At the recent Bridal Market in New York City, there were no pants suits or tuxedos on display. There is a proven demand and an affluent market for this attire.

Tips for Planners Working With Lesbian Brides

- Don't pass judgment based on the choices they make.
- Don't assume that one or both partners will wear a wedding dress or gown. Instead ask, "What are you wearing?"
- Research bridal shops that are gay-friendly or gay-owned so you can pass on a good referral.
- Identify a local gay-friendly or gay-owned business that can make a custom suit.
- Identify a local gay-friendly or gay-owned business that can tailor the heck out of a man's suit to fit a woman's figure.
- Identify gay-friendly or gay-owned businesses (either brick and mortar or online) that can sell a high-quality ready-to-wear white or black suit or tuxedo for a woman.

Tips for Bridal Salon Owners (and Planners Who Are Looking to Gather Good Vendor References)

When a bride walks into your bridal salon, please don't assume that she's marrying a man. This will cause immediate stress. Here are some tips for working with lesbian brides as they shop for wedding gowns and dresses:

- As you get to know the client, ask open-ended and gender-neutral questions rather than saying something like, "So, is the groom wearing a suit or tux?" An alternative statement would be, "Tell me about your fiancée's outfit", because fiancée is a gender neutral term when spoken.
- Understand that many couples will shop together, which may make for a very emotional experience.
- You may occasionally encounter lesbian brides or bridegrooms who are looking for a very nice suit rather than a dress. Carry a product you can offer that is fit for a woman's body, or have a tailor you can recommend for alterations.
- Don't assume that the couple has a wedding party. Many couples do not plan to have anyone standing with them during the ceremony.

- You may start to notice that lesbian brides tend to look for a simpler dress or gown, most likely without a long train or bustle. Instead of traditional bridal gowns, consider directing them towards bridesmaids' dresses in the color of their choice.

Because most gay grooms' wedding attire still follows the expected gender norms, you may not encounter the emotional minefield surrounding gender expectations until you work with a lesbian couple.

For instance, one day I was at a designer's studio taking a bride to be fitted for a custom pantsuit. Things were going really well, and we made a follow up appointment. Later that week, the bride's fiancée called me asking to cancel the second appointment with the clothing designer. Why? Because the bride's 87-year-old mother said to her, "You better not be dressed like a man on your wedding day."

So instead of wearing a custom suit that she felt the most comfortable in, she spent the next week searching for a wedding dress... and she looked and felt like a fish out of water during the process. I took her to places where the wedding dresses were simpler (like J. Crew), but we didn't have any luck finding her something she'd be comfortable in and that's because she'd be more comfortable in a suit.

The traditional wedding dress hoopla is all about uber-femininity. When a woman has a more masculine gender presentation and style, she can feel completely awkward and out of place in a bridal salon and in a traditional dress. Be very sensitive to these emotions—this is where your vendor referrals will be most appreciated!

Transgender Brides and Grooms

In the example of another client, her sex at birth was male. Her identity is female. Her sexual orientation is lesbian. She is an MTF. How does this factor into wedding planning? A few things to note:

- If you are a wedding planner and are screening vendors and scheduling appointments for this client, tell vendors in advance that your client is transgender; even if they are comfortable with the L, G and B couples, they may not be comfortable with the T.
- It's impolite to ask about the transgender client's former name or life prior to transitioning genders.
- Wedding attire shopping may be complicated, and there may be extra sensitivity in the dressing room. For example, when wedding dress shopping, my client was concerned that her shoulders were too broad for a strapless dress.

Fourteen

Because I saw that it was a giant problem to find attractive wedding suits over the years, I was committed to finding a solution. When I met fashion designer Marialexandra Garcia, a partnership was born. We created a line of ready-to-wear suits, tuxes and accessories just for lesbian weddings!

Right now, you can buy the clothes online at www.FourteenStyle.com and find a great selection of clothes in standard and boy fits, in sizes from 0-22. Everything was designed with, tested and fitted on people just like us. The fabrics are very wedding-appropriate — we even have clothes in velvet and linen.

CHAPTER 6 ACTION STEPS

☐ Find at least one retail establishment where lesbian and transgender brides and bridegrooms can comfortably have a custom tuxedo made, or a men's tuxedo altered. Ask screening questions such as, "What is your experience with same-sex weddings?" or make a statement like, "I just read this awesome book – the Business of Gay Weddings. Have you ever worked on a same-sex wedding?" Trust your instinct when you hear the responses.

☐ Find at least one store where lesbian and transgender brides can "come out" and comfortably shop for a dress. Ask screening questions.

CHAPTER 7

The Ceremony

24% of same-sex couples used a religious leader as their officiant but only 12% of same-sex marriages were held in religious spaces. I'm commonly asked why so few same-sex marriages occur in places of worship rather than simply at the reception site.

The answer is easy: not many religions accept same-sex marriages. you about this. On many occasions, I've had to call around to local churches and specifically ask, "Do you allow gay marriages to be held in your church?" Here's a quick LGBT religious guide for you in case a couple inquires (hopefully this will help avoid some pretty awkward conversations) – but check out www.GayChurch. org for specific churches in your area:

Faiths That Allow Same-Sex Marriages

- **United Church of Christ:** The United Church of Christ was the first mainstream Christian church to fully support same-sex marriage and perform marriage ceremonies.
- **Quaker Church:** The willingness to perform gay marriages varies by meetinghouse, but there is some acceptance and performance of same-sex marriages among Quakers.
- **Metropolitan Community Church**
- **Unitarian Universalist Church**
- **Unity Church**

Faiths That Limit Same-Sex Marriages

• **Episcopal:** In the Episcopal Church, priests are authorized to bless same-sex wedding ceremonies but cannot declare the marriage official or sign the marriage license. Episcopal priests in eastern Massachusetts and New York can fully marry same-sex couples without restrictions.
• **Lutheran:** Each individual church can decide whether or not to allow same-sex marriage ceremonies.
• **Congregational:** Again, the decision is left to the individual church.

Faiths That Prohibit Same-Sex Marriages

• **Baptists:** Southern Baptist and Conservative Baptist churches will not conduct same-sex marriages, nor will they allow them to be held in their churches. Certain American Baptist churches are open and inclusive.
• **Methodist**
• **Catholic**
• **Presbyterian**

Judaism
There are many branches of Judaism, and some will recognize same-sex marriages and others will not. Also, this can vary by community and rabbi as well.
• Orthodox Judaism will not recognize same-sex marriages.
• Reconstructionist and Reform Judaism do recognize it.
• Conservative Judaism is deeply divided. Some synagogues will welcome and accept it, and others will not.

I've worked with many Jewish couples over the years, or couples with one Jewish partner. Many Jewish couples (even those who are not particularly religious) incorporate Jewish wedding traditions into their same-sex wedding. It's not uncommon to see elements such as a chuppah, Kiddush cup, breaking of the glass and horah. I love a great big horah, with both brides or both grooms up on chairs – it's such a fun tradition!

But in a same-sex wedding, who stomps the glass? Traditionally it's the groom. Well, as with many things, it's up to the couple. I am a fan of one glass, two feet, but I've also seen two glasses and two feet.

Polytheistic Religions (Including Hinduism, Buddhism, and Sikhism)
Because of the very nature of these religions—multiple Gods and cultural beliefs—there isn't a doctrinal orthodoxy to follow regarding same-sex marriages. Often, it comes down to conservative cultural prohibitions rather than any religious or doctrinal problem. Also, there isn't an equivalent system of clergy hierarchy; therefore, if a gay couple can find a Hindu officiant who is willing to do the ceremony, then it is completely accepted.

NUTS AND BOLTS—THE GAY WEDDING TRADITIONS

This section introduces trends that are becoming same-sex wedding traditions. Of course, not every gay wedding will follow these traditions, but your familiarity with them will endear you to your clients.

Getting Ready Together

Instead of the "girls" and "boys" getting ready separately, most same-sex couples get ready together before the wedding. In fact, 98% of male couples and 91% of female couples get ready together. The two brides have their hair and makeup done together. If there are attendants, they gather together to get ready and celebrate. It's the pre-party! Formal photos (even with family) are taken before the ceremony so that once the wedding officially starts, there are no interruptions for formal pictures. That way, cocktail hour is spent enjoying cocktails and hors d'oeuvres.

Why is this?

Partners are often each other's best friend and closest confidante. They value each other's opinion, and they want to enjoy the little quiet moments together before they're officially married. Gay wedding ceremonies are often in the same location as the reception, and that ceremony time often cuts into the standard five-hour rental, thereby reducing the length of the reception (sometimes couples will book the space for an additional hour). With such a short reception, why sacrifice any of it for formal photos?

Jubilance and Celebration

To this day, there is nothing more moving to me than seeing a gay or lesbian couple stand up in front of their friends and family and get legally married. The validation and support they receive from their guests is truly priceless. The key word is validation. Gay weddings are jubilant. There is a sense of triumph, and I feel like there is no greater party.

What creates this sense of jubilance?

Some same-sex couples are blessed with the same amount of familial and community support as the happiest heterosexual couples. Others may be grieving the loss of support from homophobic and unsupportive families or may have experienced significant discrimination in their personal and professional lives. While it is a mistake to assume that all LGBT couples have struggled with their families, the fact still remains that federal law, as well as the majority of state laws, prohibits recognition of these marriages. In the face of this civil and legal discrimination, an LGBT wedding stands at the forefront of history and social justice, creating a sense of triumph and jubilance that is unique to gay weddings.

Pre-Wedding Champagne

As we just mentioned, there's a strong and palpable feeling of triumph and celebration at gay weddings. However, many of the guests who have never attended a gay wedding initially don't know what to expect. The guests may start out with a great deal of anticipation, nervousness, and excitement. We like to help them relax.

Traditionally at a gay wedding, guests are greeted before the ceremony with champagne and sparkling water. This can last anywhere from five to thirty minutes before the ceremony begins, and it sets the tone of something a little bit different but definitely celebratory and fun. The pre-ceremony drinks or festivities let your guests know that this wedding will be different. That it will be fun, and yes, that we're taking a bit of the edge off from the start.

Processional Options

Once the processional begins, it is not your typical wedding march: bridal chorus or trumpet voluntary, a massive wedding party, and the bride the last one to walk down the aisle, all eyes on her.

But at a gay wedding, who's the bride? Sometimes there are none and sometimes one of the women is a bridegroom! You never know what you're going to get, so let's take the emphasis away from the gender role of all eyes on the last bride down aisle. Many gay and lesbian couples who are marrying have been together for years and don't want the tradition of being walked down the aisle by other family members.

Instead, the couple may walk down a central aisle together holding hands. Or there may be two aisles with each partner processing simultaneously.

f there is no central aisle, as is often the case, the couple walks in from two different directions each accompanied by their family and/or wedding party, and they come together in the middle.

While this two-aisle gay wedding tradition can be difficult for the photographer (who will need an assistant to capture both moments in the spotlight), it provides a joyful feeling of togetherness and strength.

Music

Traditionally in a same-sex wedding, processional and recessional music is not classical but rather contemporary, even pop tunes. Sometimes these are performed live and sometimes they are recorded. A few examples we've seen lately are:

"Finally" by Ce Ce Peniston
"I'm Yours" by Jason Mraz
"Wedding Bell Blues" by Laura Nyro
"Today" by Joshua Radin
"Viva la Vida" by Coldplay

Ceremonial Elements

Following the processional, the guests remain standing, champagne in hand, for the opening remarks and tradition of "Validation & Affirmation," which is a blessing/toast between the guests and the couple. This sets the scene to help guests relax and is also how the champagne and sparkling water is used!

As with all ceremonies, the religious and secular components will vary from couple to couple. The officiant often personalizes a same-sex ceremony by talking about the history of the couple, which creates a unique and intimate atmosphere.

Later in the ceremony, after the vows are exchanged, the officiant asks the couple to sign the Foundation Covenant sacred certificate. This document is inspired by the Jewish Ketubah, Quaker wedding certificates, and other sacred documents. Here are some examples:

Typically the couple recesses out to a contemporary/pop song and departs for a yichud (based on the Jewish tradition of taking some alone time after the ceremony) while the guests sign the Foundation Covenant as witnesses to the marriage. The Covenant can also conveniently serve as a guest book and is often later framed as art.

Within the ceremony, there is often an acknowledgment of the historical significance of same-sex marriage. The following excerpt from the court ruling that first legalized same-sex marriage has become the most popular reading for gay wedding ceremonies because of its tremendous meaning. It is beautifully written by Judge Margaret Marshall from the Massachusetts State Supreme Court, and it speaks volumes about the significance of a marriage.

Marriage is a vital social institution. The exclusive commitment of two individuals to each other nurtures love and mutual support; it brings stability to our society. For those who choose to marry, and for their children, marriage provides an abundance of legal, financial, and social benefits. In return it imposes weighty legal, financial, and social obligations.... Without question, civil marriage enhances the "welfare of the community." It is a "social institution of the highest importance." ...Marriage also bestows enormous private and social advantages on those who choose to marry. Civil marriage is at once a deeply personal commitment to another human being and a highly public celebration of the ideals of mutuality, companionship, intimacy, fidelity, and family.... Because it fulfills yearnings for security, safe haven, and connection that express our common humanity, civil marriage is an esteemed institution, and the decision whether and whom to marry is among life's momentous acts of self-definition.

Written by the Massachusetts Supreme Judicial Court in their ruling Goodridge v. the Massachusetts Department of Public Health, November 2003.

Another reading gaining in popularity is an excerpt from another court ruling, this one written by Judge Vaughn Walker in his August 2010 ruling to overturn Proposition 8 in California:

Marriage is the state recognition and approval of a couple's choice to live with each other, to remain committed to one another and to form a household based on their own feelings about one another and to join in an economic partnership and support one another and any dependents. ...

The right to marry has been historically and remains the right to choose a spouse and, with mutual consent, join together and form a household. Race and gender restrictions shaped marriage during eras of race and gender inequality, but such restrictions were never part of the historical core of the institution of marriage.

Today, gender is not relevant to the state in determining spouses' obligations to each other and to their dependents. Relative gender composition aside, same-sex couples are situated identically to opposite-sex couples in terms of their ability to perform the rights and obligations of marriage under California law. Gender no longer forms an essential part of marriage; marriage under law is a union of equals...

They seek the mutual obligation and honor that attend marriage... seek recognition from the state that their union is 'a coming together for better or for worse, hopefully enduring, and intimate to the degree of being sacred.

I Now Pronounce You...

I was emailing with a couple recently who sent me a note on their ceremony draft. One of the grooms wrote, "Jeff and I have been together for more than fourteen years. After a life of saying 'my partner' I'd love, at long last, to say, 'my spouse.'"

And so he did. Language is a funny thing. I know another unmarried gay couple who have been together for more than ten years, yet who refer to themselves as lovers, not as partners. That term is not for everyone, but it works for them.

This is a big decision for gay and lesbian couples. I get asked all the time about how the officiant will declare them at the conclusion of the ceremony. I now declare you...

- legally married
- lawfully married
- partners for life
- married partners
- husbands/wives to one another
- spouses for life
- [something else?]

Jen and I chose "legally married," and that felt right for me in particular because the legal bit is so important. We live in a state where our marriage is legal, and I wanted the word "marriage" to be heard loudly and clearly. But that's not everyone's preference, and some people don't want the declaration to sound as overtly "political."

Name Changes

As with straight couples, gay couples have many different options regarding their name changes.

Today, many married couples do not change their names, or they come up with creative alternatives to the traditional expectation that the wife takes the husband's surname. But aside from the frustrations of bureaucratic offices and juggling the bazillion joint accounts, the married name change is expected and accepted by all levels of government.

One of the questions I am frequently asked by my out-of-state clients is how to change their names after marriage. Here in New York, you write your new last name on your marriage application. Then the certified copy you receive will have the new name. That certified copy is accepted by the Social Security administration and the DMV. This simple process that married straight couples experience works in other states where gay marriage is legal as well. But what happens when a couple who does not live in a marriage equality state couple returns to their home state and wants to change their name?

Couples who live in states that don't allow or recognize same-sex marriage or civil unions can't just rely on a marriage certificate as proof of a name change. Instead, they have to go through the in-court name-change process. This means they will have to pay a $100 to $400 fee to file a petition in court, publish a notice in a local newspaper, and get a court order (hoping for a gay-friendly judge) to officially change their name. Only then can they start the process of going to the DMV and calling credit card companies and other administrative offices. (Just one more area where being gay can be more expensive.)

Even more troubling, couples who live in states that DO allow or recognize same-sex marriage and civil unions sometimes don't have it much easier. While changing a name on a driver's license can be done without a problem in such states, changing federal documentation can be trickier. The marriage certificate does count as a legal document for a name change; however, there are many reports of misunderstanding and misinformation at passport and Social Security offices, and if your home state does not recognize the legal marriage, it becomes even more difficult.

So what are these couples changing their names to? I've seen hyphenated last names, such as my wife's name, Jennifer Coveney-Smith. I've seen non-hyphenated names such as mine, Bernadette Coveney Smith (yes, we did something different). I've seen one partner take the other's last name. But I love it when same-sex couples invent entirely new names, some of which were not remotely similar to either of the old names. That's kind of fun as they begin a new life together, they do so with a new name.

Examples:
Old names: Caulfield and Stansberry
New last name: Stansfield (merging Caulfield and Stansberry)

Old names: Zeitlin and Sakash
New name: Zash

What does this mean for you in the wedding industry? First, don't assume that you'll know what the couple is doing. Second, address them with their new last names in post-wedding correspondence. Third, be mindful that it's much easier for a legally married individual to change his or her name than for someone who is not legally married.

CHAPTER 7 ACTION STEPS

☐ Find at least 3 gay-owned or gay-friendly officiants in your service area. Ask screening questions such as, "What is your experience with same-sex weddings?" or make a statement like, "I just read this awesome book – the Business of Gay Weddings. Have you ever worked on a same-sex wedding?" Trust your instinct when you hear the responses.

☐ Find churches in your area that will officiate same-sex marriage ceremonies. Ask screening questions.

CHAPTER 8

The Reception

A party is a party and when it's a big wedding, you may not see many differences between gay and straight wedding receptions. Keep in mind, however, that many same-sex couples don't have big weddings.

THE INTIMATES

Think about it. If the couple has already been together for 25 years and may have had a civil union or commitment ceremony years ago, they might not want a big wedding do-over. This time, they may have a small civil ceremony and then dinner with their 20 favorite people. When same-sex marriage becomes legal in a new state or destination, much of the business goes to hotels for guest rooms who travel in to witness the legal ceremony and to restaurants which often host these smaller wedding receptions.

These small receptions might be more like a fantastic dinner party, as opposed to a typical cocktail hour, dinner and dancing. When there are 30 guests, dancing gets a little awkward!

With this small reception, we might have a tasting menu with beverage pairings. We might have live music — perhaps a small jazz band for 3 hours. We may have more toasts, or a roast. We want this to be exquisite and memorable, a truly amazing dinner. If you work a wedding venue, think about what space is appropriate for this wedding size. If you work at a hotel, maybe you can create a wedding package perfect for these intimate weddings. What part of the hotel can accommodate this wedding without interfering with your big wedding business?

ADDITIONAL ENTERTAINMENT

Same-sex couples are almost universally going to skip lots of wedding traditions. You are probably not going to see big introductions of the whole wedding party. You are probably not going to see a garter or bouquet toss. You might not even see a cake cutting or formal, announced dances with parents.

I was sitting with clients last week and we were talking about the flow of their wedding. I have this four-page questionnaire I go through a few months before the wedding with our big wedding clients. The conversation went something like this:

Me: Are you having a first dance?
Them: Nope
Me: Are you having anything tossed? Garter and bouquet are the typical things.
Them: No
Me: Are you dancing with your parents at all in any formal, announced way?
Them: No

Me: Are you cutting anything on the dessert display (this wedding has no wedding cake)?
Them: No

All of these are fairly common answers when we're planning a gay wedding, though. After all, those are traditional elements and many of our clients love the opportunity to be non-traditional and reinvent what weddings should look like!

The problem with those answers is that when we take out so many things, there is a lot of dead space and time. The guests might get bored, and heaven forbid that the wedding end early. I believe it's very important to add things back in that are conversation starters and memory makers.

Here are some examples of non-traditional wedding events that have worked well:

- photobooth pictures (the obvious example)
- drag kings/queens
- dance performance (fire dancer, salsa dancers, tango dancers, burlesque, etc.)
- caricature artist
- casino games such as a poker table
- psychic, fortune teller or tarot card reader
- cigar bar (if the venue allows it)
- aerial artist a la Cirque du Soleil

The experience doesn't have to detract from the wedding or the time spent on the dance floor. If it's a performance, keep it short (1-2 songs maximum) and upbeat and appropriate.

Special Notes for Bands and DJs

NEVER play "When a Man Loves a Woman" at a gay wedding!

That's the obvious one – but also keep an eye out for very traditional, heterosexist songs and make sure you have no slip-ups! Other quick notes:

- In many cases, the gay wedding ceremony will be in the same place as the reception, and the ceremony space will be turned over during cocktail hour to get ready for dinner. Setup of the DJ will need to happen either before the ceremony or quickly during cocktail hour. Setup for the band will have to happen during cocktail hour with some light setup before the ceremony.
- Often, the DJ or band may be asked to play or perform ceremony music, because the processional and recessional songs may be contemporary/pop songs rather than traditional classical pieces.
- You should be prepared to offer your clients a list of pop songs you think would be suitable for a processional and a recessional.
- There probably won't be a large wedding party (if there is one at all). In some cases, the DJ may be required to splice or fade a song to fit a shorter processional time.
- Because there is usually a very small or no wedding party, the announcement or introduction will likely be just of the newlyweds. In many cases, there are no parent-child dances, and the only structured dance is the first dance for the couple.
- In most cases, there is no garter or bouquet toss.
- In almost 50% of my weddings, there isn't even a cake cutting.

Special Notes for Photographers

Most couples will get ready together, so the formal photographs can be taken before the ceremony instead of during cocktail hour. Now, that's what most couples do, but I've had several couples (fewer than ten, and all women) choose to wait to see each other and have the "first look" captured by the photographer.

Do not assume what your clients want to do. Simply ask, *"Are you getting ready together?"* and *"Will there be formal photos taken before the wedding ceremony?"* These open-ended questions will get you the information you need without making anyone feel uncomfortable.

A few things to note for photographers who are shooting gay weddings:

> • Getting ready together means that there are some great opportunities for intimate photos, and I always encourage my clients to book the photographer for long enough to get that coverage.
> • This means that you might not capture that wonderful "first look" photo.
> • Many gay couples have their formal photos taken before the wedding rather than during cocktail hour, so they have time to enjoy drinks and relax. Also, if the ceremony and reception are in the same location, the rental period is often still five hours (as opposed to five hours just for the reception). I like to keep my couples present and engaged during that entire time, rather than have them whisked away for up to an hour for photos.
> • Gay couples often process down two aisles during the gay wedding ceremony, or walk in from two different directions. This is important because a site visit is a good idea in order to determine where to stand so you can pivot to capture both partners' processional. If you can't identify a good position, you may consider speaking with your client about hiring a second shooter.
> • Finally, gay wedding receptions are an exercise in omission rather than addition. You'll notice very few formal dances, no bouquet or garter toss, and sometimes not even a cake cutting. This means more fun for you and more time to capture the candid photos that truly capture the emotion of a wedding.

For even more information for photographers, check out the book, Capturing Love: The Art of Lesbian and Gay Wedding Photography by Thea Dodds and Kathryn Hamm. In addition, there's a course on gay and lesbian wedding photography taught by photographer Kristin Korpos. More information at www.GayWeddingInstitute.com/Photographers

How to Think Outside of the Box

• Whether you are a wedding planner, catering manager, florist, or hotel manager, when you work with LGBT wedding clients, you will need to check your industry assumptions at the door and be willing to be creative, flexible, and open. This training will give you a set of tools and information to use as guides, but most importantly, you should cultivate your professional mindset to think outside the typical wedding box.

• While we have heard of extremely conservative and traditional gay weddings, they happen very rarely. Think about it this way—most heterosexual couples start planning their wedding with a very full script about how it is "supposed" to look. This script comes from religion, families, ethnic culture, and Hollywood. Even the most DIY couples reference this script by rebelling against it. But in a world where same-sex marriage is still mostly illegal, who writes the script? The couples and their communities do. Imagine the freedom that comes with being able to write the screenplay of your own wedding day. Parents and grandparents may never have been to a gay wedding before—so they are hard pressed to come up with expectations that must be lived up to!

• Yes, as we've shared above, there are gay wedding traditions. And yes, many same-sex couples will choose many of the traditional elements of straight weddings. But as a wedding industry professional, imagine yourself into this state of scriptlessness. Of course, you have to retain your professional judgment about things that work and things that don't. Because we are in the wedding industry, we tend to forget the real meanings of the symbols and traditions included in the general wedding script. Sometimes these meanings are beautiful and inspiring, but sometimes they can be constricting and narrow.

FINDING VENDORS TO SERVICE YOUR SAME-SEX WEDDING

You now know that in 29 states a wedding photographer can tell a same-sex couple, "I won't photograph your wedding because you're gay" – and that's perfectly legal. Don't assume that your most frequently referred vendors are on the same page as you. Every week there is a news story about a same-sex couple being discriminated against:

- The bride in New Jersey whose bridal salon refused service when they realized she was a lesbian
- The gay couple in Texas denied a venue
- The gay couple in Seattle denied wedding flowers
- The lesbian couple in Oregon denied wedding cake

And on it goes. There was even a limousine company in Annapolis, Maryland that gave up $50,000 of annual revenue by choosing to no longer serve weddings (straight or gay). They knew that by providing transportation for straight weddings only, they would be breaking the law (because Maryland's anti-discrimination law happens to include sexual orientation).

This is a cautionary tale about the necessity of screening vendors. If you've never worked with same-sex couples, but you do work with multiple vendors and business in the wedding industry, you probably screen vendors for quality, timeliness, and value. From this moment on, you must also screen them for homophobia and heterosexism.

Don't assume that your favorite florist won't make an unwelcome or offensive remark. Many same-sex couples have wedding planning horror stories that begin with: "You'd never believe the person I just spoke to at so-and-so" as they proceed to recount an ugly story about a wedding vendor's awkwardness or distaste for the "gay lifestyle."

If you are a wedding planner and want to start marketing yourself to gay and lesbian couples, you absolutely must identify a list of gay-friendly vendors in your area. You must ask them the hard questions about their experience with gay couples, and you must use your instincts to determine whether or not they are telling you what you want to hear because they want the business. You must ask how comfortable their entire staff is —not just the person who cashes the check. The owner of the catering company might be thrilled to book a gay wedding — but how about the banquet captain? The owner of the limo company may be elated — but how about the driver? Verify that everyone on the team is open to LGBT weddings.

This is critical to your success in this market. Your reputation would be ruined if you had to kick a DJ (or any other vendor) out of a gay wedding for being hostile toward the guests. That said, as you are creating your list, start with the people you already know and trust, and build from there. If you already know 5 great gay-friendly wedding photographers, then you probably need not look any further in that category. But be sure to build that special referral list.

If you are having difficulties with your own referral list, then start doing independent research. You can start to look up gay-friendly vendors on a website like GayWeddings.com or EquallyWed.com to see which vendors are advertising in your area. However, be careful because those two websites let anyone advertise — they don't screen to make sure the business is, in fact, gay-friendly. That is still your job.

BUT I'M NOT GAY...

One of the questions I am frequently asked by my straight peers in the industry is, "Am I going to have any luck getting same-sex couples to hire me, when I'm straight?" The answer is simple: if you are great at your job and treat everyone with respect and kindness, then yes, you will get business from same-sex couples. Just because someone is gay does not make them good at their job. There are many gay-owned businesses in the world providing inferior service. A same-sex couple would rather hire an amazingly talented wedding photographer who is straight than a mediocre one who is gay.

LGBT-Owned and -Friendly Vendors and Partners
When you are working with a same-sex couple, they will want referrals from other vendors or businesses that are LGBT-owned and -friendly. For instance, if you are a wedding planner, are you referring your same-sex clients to TAG

Approved® venues? (For that matter, why not refer all your clients to TAG Approved® venues?) If you work for a hotel chain or a boutique hotel, do you have the TAG approval?

What Qualifies a Property to be TAG Approved®?

- Enforce non-discriminatory policies including "sexual orientation."
- Treat heterosexual and domestic partners equally in personnel policies.
- Provides LGBT diversity and sensitivity training for employees.
- Empower customers and employees to be "watchdogs" of its gay and lesbian business practices.
- Gives back to their community.
- Employs staff who reflect the diversity of their community.

You can find out more about this process and the standards by going to www.tagapproved.com.

CHAPTER 8 ACTION STEPS:

☐ Find at least 3 gay-owned or gay-friendly photography studios in your service area. Ask screening questions such as, "What is your experience with same-sex weddings?" or make a statement like, "I just read this awesome book – the Business of Gay Weddings. Have you ever worked on a same-sex wedding?" Trust your instinct when you hear the responses. Do NOT assume that people are gay-friendly!

☐ Find at least 3 gay-owned or gay-friendly DJs/Bands in your service area. Ask screening questions.

☐ Find local (if possible) resources for gay wedding greeting cards and gay wedding cake toppers.

CHAPTER 9

Marketing to Same-Sex Couples

The world is moving in this inclusive direction – and so is the wedding industry. More and more mainstream wedding blogs and magazines are including LGBT couples alongside their straight counterparts. Your business needs to keep up and also be integrated and inclusive.

ASSESSMENT: RISK, COURAGE, AND AUTHENTICITY

We all know that we can't be every couple's planner, photographer, DJ, venue, etc. There is enough business to go around. We have to pre-qualify our clients to make sure that they find the right fit, and that we do too. And we have to know our target market. Once we do, we can create a specific marketing strategy. Many of you are re-evaluating your marketing strategy, and you are asking yourselves these questions: "Should I begin marketing to gay and lesbian couples? Should I start working on gay weddings?"

It's fair to say no. Your business might not be ready to shift marketing strategies. You may live in a conservative area or have a very traditional client base. Marketing to gay couples and working on gay weddings can involve risk, and that requires **authentic** courage and **authentic** action.

Whatever your choice is and whatever the reason for your choice, I will not be personally offended. The reality is that it's a business decision, and if you don't want to reach this market, someone else will.

My goal with this book is teach you how to be inclusive in a way that doesn't change your brand or your identity, and that helps you *and* helps gay and lesbian couples without alienating your primary heterosexual market. It can be done. The first rule is: be authentic. If you are authentic, you will not alienate your existing client base.

MARKETING: THE KEY TO EVERYTHING

The first priority in attracting and retaining same-sex couples as clients is the couple's experience and interactions with your business.

An incredibly close second priority is your marketing materials.

Did you know that it takes less than two seconds for a potential client/consumer to form a first impression of your business and product? And did you know that once that first impression is formed—for better or worse—it is almost impossible to change? Advertising executives know this, which is why they spend so much money on crafting and designing the perfect marketing strategy and materials.

Some fast facts about marketing to same-sex couples:

- 78% of couples want to work with businesses that specifically advertise to them
- 86% of couples find it somewhat or very important to work with businesses that have gender-neutral marketing language and photos
- 79% find it very or somewhat important to work with businesses that have been trained about gay weddings

Your Target Market
Who is your target market? Chances are, it's not every single LGBT couple that's getting hitched. Try to be more specific and narrow down the possibilities. Do

you prefer working with men or women? What age? In what industries do your ideal clients work? In which neighborhoods do they live?

Dig deeper. What magazines do they like to read? What do they do on weekends? Are they politically active? A very specific profile of your target market will help you create the most accurate marketing campaign.

(By the way, this is a great exercise for marketing to your straight audience as well.)

If you work for a wedding venue, think about what type of client your venue attracts. If you have amazing woodwork and stunning Tiffany chandeliers you will attract a different client than a raw loft space. This will help inform your target market.

A GENERATIONAL COMPARISON

Just as with the straight population, there are generational differences between younger and older same-sex couples. Comparing the two may inform your target market and thus your advertising strategies.

Millennials

- At least one set of parents will be involved, sharing their opinions and expectations even if they are not paying for much, if any, of the wedding
- The couple grew up in an age when gay marriage is part of their expected journey (the first U.S. state legalized gay marriage in 2004)
- As a result, this couple may not be very aware of the more discriminatory laws and policies around gay marriage and the additional steps necessary to further protect their families
- This is typically the first marriage for both and no children are involved

• The couple is more aware of access to planning resources (especially online) and will turn to wedding magazines and blogs for information and inspiration

• This couple may have a lower budget because of the lack of parental support and less time in the workforce

• This couple's wedding likely will be more similar to a traditional straight wedding (not that there's anything wrong with that!)

• This couple is less tolerant of accidental heterosexism. They expect you to know better.

Generation X/Baby Boomers

• May have already had a commitment ceremony, civil union or other event — or all of the above!

• Very little, if any, parental involvement in the decision-making process

• Pay for the entire wedding themselves

• May have been previously married to members of the opposite sex

• May have children from those previous straight marriages

• Have a strong appreciation of the legality of their gay marriage

• Have a deep appreciation of YOU as a vendor and your kindness to them as a same-sex couple

• A willingness to be less traditional in their gay wedding ceremony

• A wedding reception that may be more of an elegant formal dinner party than a typical one with dancing

• Often plan their wedding closer to the actual date

• Have smaller weddings, with fewer than 100 guests, often fewer than 50

• This couple is more tolerant of accidental heterosexism because they are used to it!

TWO MARKETING OPTIONS

You can approach your marketing in two ways. Your decision is personal and depends on how much you're willing to risk in potentially alienating some of your current client base. But also, remember that a higher risk often means a higher rate of return. This training will guide you in both directions. This isn't an "all or nothing" situation—your marketing plan will be personalized to your business needs and the climate of your state and community, and it may involve elements from both options.

> **Option 1:** Proactively market to LGBT couples by advertising on gay-wedding websites and by using direct language in your marketing materials.

> **Option 2:** Quietly erase the heterosexism from your business through inclusive and neutral strategies without being explicit.

STRATEGIES FOR EVERYONE

Marketing Materials: Denaturalizing What Feels Natural to Your Business and Rebuilding a New Natural

How to Lose $30,000 in Thirty Seconds

One day, two brides who were in the process of booking their wedding venue called me after visiting a venue's website. I went to the website and read the first sentence of the first paragraph on the weddings page: "Toast the Bride and the Groom from the terrace with its view of the surrounding hills."

But can we toast just the brides?
Or can we toast just the grooms?

That's what this lesbian couple called me to find out. Is this a gay-friendly venue? They'd have to come out to the venue and ask that question themselves. It's not unusual to feel nervous about the process of calling, asking, and coming out.

Is this venue willing to risk losing $30,000 on food and beverage rather than make the photos and language on their website inclusive? Are you?

Remember, heterosexism means that the cultural and interpersonal dynamics function around the heteronormative assumption that everyone is heterosexual. If someone is heterosexist, it doesn't make them a bad person, nor does it mean that they are prejudiced against LGBT people. But it does mean that the same-sex couple is excluded from these assumptions, and therefore, they have to "come out" and educate people over and over again. Heterosexism assumes heterosexuality as the norm, and positions LGBT people as non-normative and the exceptions to the rule. Most people are unconsciously heterosexist.

Heterosexist conversations during gay wedding planning are awkward for the couple and also awkward and potentially embarrassing for the vendor. However, if you begin to question your daily assumptions, retrain your reactions, and recalibrate your perceptions of what is normal, you can avoid these types of gaffes.

Heterosexism relies on assumptions and "common sense" ideas of what is normal and natural. Marketing your business to same-sex couples will require you to flip the switch to remind yourself (constantly) that sometimes there are two brides or two grooms. In the same way that you use marketing to attract your target heterosexual couples, you will also need to fine-tune your strategies and materials to attract your new demographic.

However, this does not mean that you need to place a banner on your website or a seal on all your materials that states that you are "100% gay-friendly." In fact, if you did that and yet your forms still asked for the bride and groom's names, it would be highly offensive and reflect very poorly on your business.

Take a few moments to go through this checklist and answer it as best you can:

☐ Does your marketing material, contact form, or contract have the phrase "bride and groom" paired together?

☐ Does your marketing material, contact form, or contract have the phrase "husband and wife" paired together?

☐ Do your marketing materials reflect diversity, and not just diversity in sexual orientation? In what ways?

☐ Are your marketing materials and imagery primarily bride and female-centric?

☐ Do you use language indicating that a wedding is a girl's fairy-tale dream come true, or something similar?

☐ Do your materials assume there will be attendants and refer to them as the bridal party and the groomsmen or the bride's side and the groom's side?

Be Inclusive, Don't Alienate

Using the checklist above, the first step is to remove heterosexist language from your materials. Remember, language matters. Put yourself in your clients' positions—empathize. Suppose you are a bride filling out a form that asks for the groom's name. What would you do? Cross out the word "Groom" and write "BRIDE" in capital letters? Would you feel disheartened and more than a little irritated that you are spending a lot of money at a business whose forms have no place for your marriage? It is very likely that you would have a strong emotional response, whether it is anger, sadness, frustration, or impatience. And with that emotional response comes a business decision—as a client, do you really want to spend your money here?

Here are the first steps to take in eliminating this hurtful and exclusive language.

In contracts and contact forms: Eliminate the use of "bride" and "groom" or "husband" and "wife" and substitute one of the following:

- Party A, Party B
- Client Name, Client Name
- Client A, Client B
- Partner A, Partner B
- Bride/Groom, Bride/Groom
- Clients Names
- Name, Name
- Wedding Couple

In general narrative, be subtle. Use plurals in your marketing materials say brides and grooms rather than bride and groom. Or use the phrase "all couples" or even just "couple" instead of "bride and groom"

Bad example:
Magnificent Affairs works with Toronto-area brides to create exquisite wedding celebrations.

Good example:
Magnificent Affairs works with Toronto-area brides and grooms to create exquisite wedding celebrations.

Now, where do you make those language changes in your materials? The Frequently Asked Questions section, under Services, About Us, your blog – everywhere! Just be inclusive.

In any checklist-type materials you have, substitute the word "wedding" for "bridal." Use an inclusive alternative word for bridesmaids and groomsmen. Look for references to dresses and tuxedos and change to "attire" or "wardrobe."

Chances are, many of your traditional couples may not even notice the shifts in language. But for same-sex couples, it will make all the difference. A more sensitive area may be your photos and visuals. Do you already have a diverse depiction of race and ethnicity in your photos? Perhaps it is time to include some photos of same-sex couples on your website and in your marketing materials or at least more photos that are non-gender specific.

Although it is an unfortunate reality, it is still the case that many heterosexual people do not feel comfortable seeing public displays of affection between same-sex couples. While we believe that a picture of two grooms sharing a kiss near their wedding cake is just as normal as showing the same picture of a bride and groom, you should use your own judgment about your clients' degrees of comfort. You are walking a fine line as a business, and it is up to you to draw the line about your inclusivity and its effects on your customers. Just because you don't want to shock your traditional clients doesn't mean you have to give up on inclusivity.

STRATEGIES FOR THOSE WHO WANT TO BE OVERTLY GAY-FRIENDLY

If you and your business are in a place where you want to proactively market to same-sex couples (as opposed to simply erasing the heterosexism from your materials), first think about this question that we are asked all the time:

What's the difference between same-sex marriage and a gay wedding? Is one more correct than the other? In marketing materials, what phrase should I use same-sex marriages, gay weddings, commitment ceremonies, civil unions, or something else?

A marriage is just that, a civil institution with certain protections and benefits. The marriage can happen at City Hall. But we're in the business of weddings. When I'm speaking about public policy and laws, I use the term same-sex marriage or gay marriage. When I speak about the celebrations, I call them weddings.

For your marketing materials, if you want to indicate that you are excited to support and work with same-sex couples, you should first think about the demographics and the reality of your service area. Consider this:

- 82% of lesbians and 74% of gay men prefer the term "gay and lesbian" over LGBT, GLBT, queer, gay-friendly and other similar terms. "LGBT" is a close second.
- If you work in a state where civil unions are legal, use that term if you want to be overt
- If you work in a state where marriage is legal, then say weddings
- Younger couples hate the term "commitment ceremonies" but older couples don't mind

Some phrases which I'd advise you not to use:

- alternative lifestyle
- alternative wedding
- holy union

Now that you've chosen the proper term, think again about your demographics and target market:

- If you use civil unions, commitment ceremonies or LGBT/same-sex/gay weddings, you'll be safe and non-offensive.
- If you use rainbows or pink triangles, you'll be seen as cheesy (more on that later).
- If the photos on your website are very heterocentric and don't reflect your modern attitude towards gay weddings, then your use of any of those phrases won't sell much. The photos tell the story.

Here are some good examples on how to use this language successfully:

Magnificent Affairs is proud to work with the Toronto area's finest couples, including gay and lesbian couples.

Magnificent Affairs is a proud supporter of marriage equality and happily plans weddings for all couples.

The Difference Between Niche Marketing and Segregation

When I was speaking about gay weddings to a group of wedding professionals recently, one of the questions I was asked was whether vendors should create one website targeting engaged straight couples and another website targeting engaged gay and lesbian couples.

I strongly advise you not to do this. Despite your best intentions, this will make you inauthentic.

Your straight clients will find the gay website and the more open-minded of those couples won't respect you because you're afraid to be openly inclusive. The less open-minded ones will also find your alternate site and may be offended. And I promise you that the gay clients will find the straight website and will think you're afraid to indicate your support of gay couples on your regular site. There's no reason you can't have one smartly written site with inclusive photos, assembled in a way as to not offend straight or gay couples. I know this is a delicate act but it can be done.

The key is to think of your marketing in terms of new clientele for your services, rather than constructing an entirely separate branch of your business. When it comes down to it, heterosexual and same-sex couples are part of the same story of love, wedding planning, celebration, and marriage. As a wedding industry professional, you are simply widening your clientele base, not changing the core of your services.

Stay Away from Tokenizing and Using Cheesy Symbols

Tokenizing is often the result of misdirected "tolerance." The concept of tolerance is an insulting one, because it implies that there is something bad/not normal/a little off/strange that the rest of the normal world should tolerate, and therefore, get kudos for "tolerating" "those types" of people.

Despite your best intentions, it's annoying to hear things like, "I went to college with a lot of gay people." I'll never forget when Jen and I were interviewing someone to be our nanny and she mentioned during our meeting, "I was bisexual in college." Hmmm. We were just not sure what to do that information. It certainly had no bearing on her ability to care for our son. But it was clearly her way of trying to relate to us. Anyway, I'd suggest that if you have something tokenizing to say, keep quiet!

If you are a wedding vendor, there is no need to put rainbows on your website. There are better ways to show your inclusivity.

Truthfully, modern gays and lesbians aren't that into rainbows. They have a lovely meaning and the meaning of the pink triangle is very powerful, but we find both symbols to be cheesy and dated. Rainbows and pink triangles aren't going to offend gays and lesbians, nor are they politically incorrect. But they are very "old school." So while you can put rainbows in your marketing materials, you might find that the modern engaged gay or lesbian couple isn't into it.

That being said, rainbows aren't all terrible. Clever uses of the rainbow flag are brilliant if executed properly, as in this cover of The New Yorker, the issue after President Obama endorsed same-sex marriage:

 If you choose to use a symbol, a more modern alternative is the Human Rights Campaign (HRC) symbol, the yellow equals sign on the blue background. You may see this on bumper stickers it's very common, and we all know what it means, at least in North America. Just make sure you're a member of HRC before using the graphic!

KicKuiKa

Photos

Just as it's important to clean up any heterosexist language in your marketing materials, it's similarly important to inspect all of your photos. I fully expect that most of your portfolio is of straight brides and grooms. That's common. Maybe you've never worked on a same-sex wedding before. That doesn't mean that your photos can't suggest otherwise.

You can organize some of the photos in these examples below in an afternoon… and if you are concerned about your straight audience, the key is ambiguity! If your website is full of very traditional poses like this, same-sex couples will not be as drawn to your work:

But that doesn't mean you should go in the other extreme. A photo like this of two guys kissing might make your straight clients uncomfortable

But these might not...

Use photos of the bride and groom as individuals to leave some element of mystery... is she marrying a man or a woman?

Include some long shots where there is room for ambiguity

Who do these bouquets belong to? Two brides, or a bride and her maid of honor?

Who do these bowties belong to?

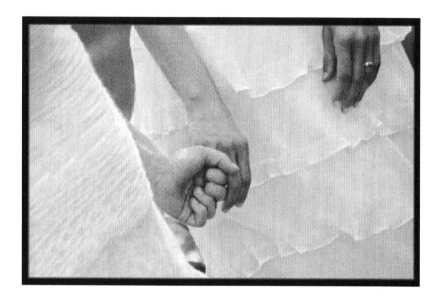

A close up shot provides some ambiguity

Print Advertising

Although this is changing, most places in the world there is no such thing as a printed gay wedding magazine. The local gay newspaper or magazine might have an annual weddings issue, but unless you live in New York City, Atlanta or Brazil, you're probably not going to find an actual printed magazine that comes out a few times a year specifically focusing on gay weddings.

That's OK. Only 23% of same-sex couples are reading wedding magazines. Gay men don't read wedding magazines much anyway, and lesbians would rather read a high quality bridal magazine, even if it's very heterosexist. If you are choosing to invest in print advertising, remember this when you choose where to advertise:

- Gay men are more likely to read gay media than wedding media
- Lesbians are more likely to read wedding media than gay media
- And most places in the world, there's nothing in between.

If you do decide to invest in print advertising, I hope you make it a thoughtful, amazing ad!

THE *WEDDINGS UNVEILED* DRAMA

If you're in the wedding industry, you may have read the story floating around Facebook and Twitter in early 2013 about Anne Almasy, the wedding photographer from Atlanta who bought an ad in Weddings Unveiled magazine, only to have that ad rejected because it showed a photo of two brides. Not one bride. Not a bride and a groom. But two brides, marrying each other.

I hate that this happened and that Anne Almasy had to have those conversations with the magazine. But I love this happened and I love that Anne Almasy had to have those conversations. Because, she, a straight woman, wrote a fantastic blog post on what happened. Her reaction and the comments and shares are starting a much needed dialogue in the wedding industry.

An excerpt from Anne's blog post:
A friend of mine asked me, "Aren't there other publications who would be happy to advertise to the gay community?" And, you know, yes, I'm quite sure there are. But I chose *Weddings Unveiled* because I'm not trying to advertise to "the gay community." I'm advertising to couples who are getting married. This couple didn't get "gay married." They didn't have a "gay wedding." They got married. They had a wedding. They share their lives, their joys and sorrows, and all the mundane daily things that we all share with our partners. They are just people. In love. Committed to one another.

After a few days of backlash, the beleaguered Weddings Unveiled editors retracted their decision and agreed to run the ad. They indicated that they personally support marriage equality, but were afraid of what their readers would think. It seems to be a common sentiment.

Submitting Your Real Weddings for Publication
Relative to the number of straight weddings featured on blogs and in wedding media, the number of gay weddings is paltry. We have to change that! There are some blogs that specialize in publishing LGBT weddings, and there are a few blogs and websites and magazines that have showcased our glorious weddings.

I would love for there to be more same-sex weddings featured right along opposite-sex weddings in wedding blogs. Here are the top same-sex wedding blogs if you choose to submit to these:

- GayWeddings.com
- EquallyWed.com
- 4RealEqualityWeddings.com
- OnaBicycleBuiltforTwo.com
- Gay.Weddings.com (TheKnot)

These major blogs have featured LGBT weddings with the "Real Weddings" tag:

- Junebug Weddings
- Offbeat Bride
- Ruffled
- Snippet and Ink
- Style Me Pretty
- Wedding Chicks
- A Practical Wedding

The following mainstream wedding magazines have featured LGBT weddings in the "Real Weddings" sections:

- Brides
- Martha Stewart Weddings
- Southern New England Weddings
- Destination Weddings & Honeymoons
- The Knot
- Vermont Vows
  BLISS CELEBRATIONS

Many of these outlets accept submissions directly through TwoBrightLights.com.

ONLINE ADVERTISING

Below is a selection of websites that many LGBT couples visit when planning their weddings.

Get familiar with the sites, the quality, the information, and see if any of your vendor partners are listed on them. On many sites, there are places for reviews—check them out to see what the buzz is about your vendors, and see which ones you may consider for your own advertising dollars.

Most of the sites below do not screen vendors to make sure they are gay-friendly. Vendors can pay to be listed even if they are not comfortable working with same-sex couples. It is your responsibility to do your due diligence when offering your list of vendors to clients—and as always, the best referral is the one that comes from your own experience.

- GayWeddings.com: the first and pioneering gay wedding directory (partnered with WeddingWire) and boutique
- EquallyWed.com: an online wedding magazine and wedding directory
- PurpleUnions: a vendor directory only, consistently on the first page of Google
- Gay.Weddings.com (by TheKnot) features real gay weddings, articles, news stories, and a vendor directory
- OnaBicycleBuiltforTwo.com: a real wedding blog with a small directory
- AVoteandaVow.com: a real wedding blog with a directory of screened vendors (free to advertise)

As you review these sites and any others you see, think back to your target market and ask yourself, "would my target market visit this website when looking for wedding vendors?" You may realize that some of these sites are not a good place for you to advertise. I only advertise my wedding business on a couple of the above sites.

Don't forget about Facebook, Pinterest and Google. Search Engine Optimization (SEO) is very important, and so is being on the first page of Google in your area, even if it means are you have set up a pay for click service, such as Google Adwords. Facebook is extremely powerful, particularly if you know your target market extremely well. For example, you can tell Facebook to only show your ad to women in Chicago who are engaged, interested in women, college graduates, between the ages of 30-40 who watch The Ellen Degeneres Show. Pretty creepy! But it works...

Online Banner Ads

If you do focus on online advertising, banner ads can be very effective. Here is my favorite:

GAY WEDDING EXPOS—WORTH IT?

I get this question all the time: *Is it worth my time and money to sign up for a booth at a "gay wedding expo" or other gay wedding show?*

It's a great question that comes down to more of a fundamental marketing strategy. Ask yourself these questions:

- Who is my target market?
- Are they male or female?
- What is my average wedding budget?

Two Bright Lights (a collaborative image publishing website) recently released data that indicated that wedding expos/shows don't generate many bookings. In fact, compared to other forms of advertising (print ads, Google, and other online listings), they're pretty much a waste of money.

So why would gay wedding expos be any different? They're not, really.

We used to have booths at expos and with a one-off exception, gave them up over three years ago. The mostly female couples who attend *(and trickle in, let's be honest)* aren't often there to commit to a purchase. When asked to participate in an expo, I always ask myself, *"would my target market be spending their Saturday at a wedding expo?"* And the answer is always no — those clients will be spending the weekend at their weekend home, not trolling for free cake!

Now, what works for you may be different. Chances are, if your business has had luck with traditional wedding expos, then you will probably do well at gay wedding expos.

PUT YOUR POLITICS WHERE YOUR BUSINESS IS

If you are serious about not only supporting equality, inclusivity, and opening your business to the LGBT community, but also gaining the respect and profit of the community, then you should put your commitment into action through your politics. Support marriage equality legislation in your state and at the federal level by joining an organization like HRC (the Human Rights Campaign) or Marriage Equality USA. Write your representatives and senators about passing the Employment Non-Discrimination Act (ENDA) and passing marriage equality legislation in your state or country.

Never underestimate the power of an individual connection or conversation—when someone expresses intolerance or big- otry or seems "on the fence" about marriage equality, share your joyful and inspiring stories about working with same-sex couples.

CHAPTER 9 ACTION STEPS:

☐ Who is your target market? Be as specific as possible.
☐ Go through the steps on the Heterosexist Checklist:

- Do your marketing materials, contact form or contract have the phrase "bride and groom" paired together?
- Do your marketing materials, contact form or contract have the phrase "husband and wife" paired together?
- Do your marketing materials reflect diversity, and not just diversity in sexual orientation?
- Does your "wedding planner" worksheet (planning timeline document) have inclusive language?
- Are your marketing materials and imagery primarily bride and female-centric?
- Do you use language indicating that a wedding is a girl's dream come true, fairytale or similar?
- Do your materials assume there will be attendants and refer to them as the bridal party or the groomsmen or the bride's side and the groom's side?
- Are all of your testimonials only of straight couples?

☐ Circle every instance of bride/groom centric language on your website & marketing materials. Substitute neutral language.
☐ Neutralize some of photos on your website & marketing materials, using examples mentioned earlier in the chapter.
☐ When you have them, add gay testimonials to your website.
☐ Make a marketing plan. Identify four concrete, sales and marketing-related action steps you'll establish as a result of this book.

CHAPTER 10

Summary

I realize I covered a lot of information and went very in-depth. I hope you read every word. If you didn't, I totally understand, so here is a summary of the key points:

1. There is a spectrum of gender, sexuality and sexual expression, not just straight and gay, male and female.

2. Avoid using these potentially offensive terms:

Homosexual
Queer
Lifestyle or Alternative Lifestyle
Sexual Preference
Special Rights
Gay Agenda
SheMale
Tranny
Transsexual

3. Be flexible and non-judgmental… you may be asked to work on the most over-the-top wedding for leather bears EVER!

4. Current states with same-sex marriage: Massachusetts, Connecticut, Vermont, Maine, New Hampshire, Iowa, Maryland, Washington, Minnesota, New York, Rhode Island, Delaware, California, Hawaii, New Jersey, Illinois (in June) and D.C. Civil unions are legal in Colorado.

5. You are your clients' advocate! Be aware of the laws in your area, only refer them to LGBT-friendly businesses, and only hire LGBT-friendly staff.

6. Don't assume that: there will be parents involved, there will be a wedding party, what the couple will wear… Don't assume anything! Ask open-ended questions.

7. Know your preferred market within the vast LGBT market. What does your ideal client look like?

8. "Gay and Lesbian" and "LGBT" are the preferred terms over things like "same-sex", "GLBT" and others.

9. Be inclusive/gender-neutral in your: contracts, marketing materials, forms. Get some more inclusive photos!

10. Rainbows are overdone and often seen as dated and cheesy, unless cleverly used.

11. If you want to work with same-sex couples, then actively support marriage equality by volunteering and aligning yourself and your business with organizations fighting for LGBT rights.

And finally, I'll end with a list that I first published on the Huffington Post in 2011. This article received about 1900 comments, with most people in disbelief that people actually say these things. Yes, yes they do – I don't make any of this stuff up!

The Top Ten Things Not to Say to an Engaged Same-Sex Couple

☐ "Which one of you is the bride?" or "Where's the bride? (to two grooms)"

☐ "Is one of you the bride and one of you the groom in this relationship?" or "Is one of you going to wear the dress and one of you wear the tux?" (said to brides and grooms)

☐ "That's not what happens at a real wedding!"

☐ "How do your parents feel about all this?"

☐ "I'm so thrilled to meet you. I'm a big fan of Ellen and I know we'll get along just great!" or "I'm so thrilled to meet you. You know, I was bisexual in college!"

☐ "I'm thrilled to be supportive of your alternative lifestyle!" or "I'm thrilled to be supportive of your sexual preference!"

☐ "Oh, is that even legal?"

☐ "Which way do you swing?" (inappropriate sexual question)

☐ "Yes, we will plan homosexual weddings here."

☐ "So will there be drag queens and show tunes at this wedding?"

Have fun with these joyful weddings... the wedding industry will never be the same. And I believe that's a very good thing!

Acknowledgments

This book is a labor of love which would not be possible without the unwavering support of my wife Jen who moved with me to New York City (a city she hates!) from Boston (a city she loves!) to support my career.

I also want to thank Alyssa Stalsberg Canelli who did a great deal of academic insight into the content I'm sharing. Thanks also to my editor, Elizabeth Seiver, and my other editor (and very dear friend) Jane Lee.

In 2009, I first met Sean Low, owner of a company called The Business of Being Creative. He told me to write down everything I've learned over the years of planning same-sex weddings, and then start talking about it, and blogging about it – because people really are craving this information. He was right. His simple statement opened a whole new world to me. So thank you, Sean, and thank you for being a longtime advocate of equal rights.

Thanks also to Rebecca Grinnals and Kathryn Arce, owners of Engaging Concepts, who encouraged me to write my first book, Gay Wedding Confidential, and provided many other amazing insights on the evolution of my business. In fact, they gave me so many good ideas that I turned into goals on which I'm still working.

Thank you for the great LGBT marketing and marriage data collected by the Williams Institute at UCLA's School of Law, Community Marketing, Inc, Witeck Communications and Harris Interactive.

Thank you to every single person who has ever read my blog, who come to one of my presentations, or taken my Gay Wedding Institute Certification Course. Thank you because of what YOU are doing to support same-sex couples in their wedding plans. Thank you for being advocates, and allies and just generally kind, open-minded people. You know, you are changing the world.

And finally, thanks to my hundreds of former clients from around the world. We are doing this for you, and people like you. You inspire me each and every day.

CHAPTER 11

Appendix

DATA

In 2013, we conducted a survey with Community Marketing & Insights, the leading LGBT research organization. We asked about what traditions were followed (or not), where couples found their team of wedding vendors, the size of their wedding party, and much more. Here are some of the notable findings:

- The economic impact for states offering civil unions or domestic partnerships is considerably less than those offering marriage. 76% of couples receiving a civil union or domestic partnership did not have a traditional wedding with ceremony and reception. The economic impact of same-sex couples getting legally married is three times greater than those receiving a civil union or domestic partnership, because married couples are far more likely to have a reception with guests or their receptions have a greater number of guests.
- Female same-sex couples spend more on their weddings than male same-sex couples. For those already married, female same-sex couples spent 15% more than the men.
- In every category tested, female same-sex couples were more likely to participate in "wedding ceremony traditions" than the men. For example 66% of women purchase engage-

ment rings vs. 19% of men. Also female same-sex couples are far more likely follow wedding traditions such as rehearsal dinners or first dances at the reception.

• 76% of same-sex couples feel it is important to work with LGBT-friendly businesses when planning their wedding.

• 24% of same-sex couples used a religious leader as their officiant but only 12% of same-sex marriages were held in religious spaces.

• 67% of newly engaged same-sex couples have emotional support around their marriage from their parents compared to only 47% of those already married. Female same-sex couples indicated more emotional support from friends, family and peers than male same-sex couples.

• 84% of male couples and 73% of female couples are paying for the wedding themselves.

• Legalizing marriage equality in the entire United States is important to 98% of same-sex couples.

• Engaged same-sex couples are projecting an average of 80 guests at their weddings

• 78% of male couples and 59% of female couples entered the ceremony space with their partner as opposed to being escorted by someone.

• 36% of lesbian couples had one partner in a suit and one in a dress; 27% had two dresses and 8% had two suits.

• 30% of same-sex couples do not have a wedding party/attendants.

• 17% of male couples and 35% of female had a bachelor/ette party.

• 9% of male couples and 29% of female had a wedding shower.

• 72% want vendors with LGBT inclusive language, and 69% LGBT inclusive photos.

SAME-SEX WEDDING PLANNING RESOURCES:

14Stories.com (our planning company)
GayWeddingInstitute.com (our training company)
FourteenStyle.com (our clothing line for lesbians)
Gay.Weddings.com
GayWeddings.com
EquallyWed.com
AVoteandaVow.com
HandHWeddings.com
LoveIncMag.com

INVITATIONS:

GayWeddings.com
TwoPaperDolls.com
LadyfingersLetterpress.com
OutVite.com
WeddingPaperDivas.com

LEGAL:

GLAD, GLAD.org
Lambda Legal, LambdaLegal.org

ADVOCACY:

Family Equality Council, familyequality.org
Freedom to Marry, freedomtomarry.org
Human Rights Campaign, HRC.org
Marriage Equality USA, marriageequality.org
National Center for Lesbian Rights, NCLRights.org
National Gay and Lesbian Task Force, NGLTF.org

MEDIA:

GLAAD, www.GLAAD.org

Made in the USA
San Bernardino, CA
14 September 2015